| AUTHOR PALMER, J. | CLASS 940.545 PAL |
|---|---|

**TITLE** Luck on my side: the diaries and
reflections of a young wartime
sail

# LUCK ON MY SIDE

# LUCK ON MY SIDE

## THE DIARIES AND REFLECTIONS OF A YOUNG WARTIME SAILOR 1939–45

by

## JOHN PALMER

LEO COOPER

First published in Great Britain in 2002 by
LEO COOPER
an imprint of Pen & Sword Books,
47 Church Street,
Barnsley
South Yorkshire,
S70 2AS

Copyright © 2002 by John Palmer

ISBN 0 85052 910 7

A CIP catalogue record for this book is
available from the British Library.

Typeset in Sabon by
Phoenix Typesetting, Burley-in-Wharfedale, West Yorkshire.

Printed in England by
CPI UK

011904168

# CONTENTS

Foreword – Admiral of the Fleet Sir Henry Leach                    xi

**Chapter**
  I    Introduction                                                 1
  II   Serving with Commodores of Convoys                           8
  III  HMS *Clematis* in the Battle of the Atlantic                22
  IV   Southbound                                                   41
  V    Life in the South Atlantic                                   43
  VI   Takoradi and Lagos                                           92
  VII  Homeward Bound                                              111
  VIII HMS *Exe* in North Africa and the
       Battle of the Atlantic                                      121
  IX   Hospital and HMS *Dryad*                                    143
  X    HMS *Amethyst*                                              145
  XI   U-Boat Surrender                                            156
  XII  Reunion after Fifty Years                                   158
       Index                                                       161

To my wife, Mary, the boating Wren, who was always such a wonderful example of the part played by Wrens and thereafter has looked after me and has inspired the sort of life of which I dreamed during those wartime years.

# Acknowledgements

Above all, I shall always be indebted to Elizabeth Morris who had been my secretary for the best part of forty years and somehow has always managed to read my illegible writing, including even the diaries which follow in this book. Without that great skill and her patient encouragement, the book would not have been possible. As well as being indebted to her, I am grateful also for the considerable help she has had from many of those in our old office, Bevan Ashford, Tiverton.

I am also indebted to Sir Robin Maxwell-Hyslop for his generous encouragement, although probably misplaced, as the one responsible for persuading me to embark on the book in the first place, but above all I am also grateful to my former shipmates, particularly my brother-in-law, John Ellyatt DSC, whose memory of the days we were together has been much better than mine, and to Douglas Mather, the First Lieutenant of *Amethyst*.

# FOREWORD
by
## Admiral of the Fleet Sir Henry Leach

This is an unusual book. It is based on the unexpurgated diaries of a young Oxford graduate whose mind was bigger than his opportunities and who served as an RNVR Officer throughout the whole of World War Two, later to become President of the Law Society.

Wisely the author has made no attempt to edit the original entries (though he has added some notes). Thus the reader is let into the thoughts of an intelligent twenty-year-old often driven to the limit of his endurance, warts and all.

In their quiet way the diaries bring the harsh events of those times vividly to life. You almost feel the relentless cold and wet of a Corvette's open bridge in the storms of the North Atlantic, the creeping exhaustion from incessant watchkeeping and lack of sleep, the horrors of torpedoed Merchant Ships, the spectacular explosions of tankers, the suicidal dash under fire towards an enemy Pocket Battleship. When the scene shifts to the coast of West Africa the thrust is temporarily reduced, but the blistering heat and humidity and the sheer monotony of endless escort work with hardly a break inexorably impair human relationships in the cramped quarters of a small ship. Cockroaches and a venomous rat do the rest. As if the growing U-boat menace was not enough, the threat from surface raiders and, during the North African landings, from the air, add to the hazards of life at sea.

The book is not at all sensational. It is a restrained, unassuming contemporary account of conditions in convoy escorts during a major war. As such it is a valuable contribution to history. I commend it to those who care to read about these things and to all those who "do business in great waters".

*Henry Leach*
AF

Admiral of the Fleet
Sir Henry Leach
February 2002

# CHAPTER I

# Introduction

My father was sure in 1937 that war with Germany was inevitable. He said I should go to Oxford as soon as I could, although it would mean doing so at seventeen. He was right. In consequence I had two years there while most of my contemporaries had only one. They were academically undistinguished years. Apart from the minimum of work, my time was spent at the Union, in politics and in sailing. In my first year Edward Heath was President of the Union and many others of those who spoke and survived the war later became national figures. My politics were then Liberal. I well remember speaking on street corners in Baldwin's constituency of Bewdley where Liberalism could hardly have been more of a lost cause. I remember Heath as a most kind and considerate President who always managed to be encouraging to those of us who spoke. I have no record of debates except one, where I still have a copy of the Cherwell report of a debate when I had spoken but I am afraid it is not very flattering. 'There then followed an amusing but totally irrelevant speech from Mr John Palmer.'

It is refreshing to reflect on how unselfconscious one was and how seriously one took oneself in those days. Sailing we took even more seriously. There was just time to sail against Cambridge in 1939 at Falmouth. Thereafter for the next six years life became rather different.

It is perhaps just worth recording that during my last year at school there was a chance to spend a term in a German school, which I did. It is difficult now and even more difficult then to think of being at what was a very Nazi school. It was a tough regime, being woken at 6.30 in the morning and ordered to run round the grounds even in deep snow. That was followed by being given two sandwiches which was all you got for breakfast but only after the swastika had been hoisted and we had all stood to attention giving the Nazi salute. I suppose I thought little of it at the time but it is a strange picture to think of, for instance, going down to the village near the school, meeting, on the way there and back,

1

schoolmasters and others to whom one had to give the Nazi salute. I did not know then how soon we would be killing each other.

Before the war, in 1938, during my second year at Oxford, I had tried to join the RNVR, but in a somewhat discouraging letter I was told by the Commanding Officer of HMS *President* that direct entry to the RNVR had ceased and that recruiting to the lower deck had also been 'discontinued for the time being'. But the University's Joint Recruiting Board was more encouraging. Surprisingly I still have both letters, which follow. I presented myself for interview on 9 September 1939. Life in the Navy then soon started.

In December six of us from Oxford joined the Royal Navy as Midshipmen RNVR. Four of us survived, two having been lost in submarines. Six also joined from Cambridge a month or two later. Some of them were lost too, but one who survived later became my brother-in-law.

Meanwhile my brother had joined the Army. At that time he was at Bletchley where he remained for the whole of the war. I had no idea what he was doing. I did not ask him and he never told me. In fact I just thought of him as having a soft job in the Army, whatever it was. After the war he went to Cheltenham. It is noteworthy that I still did not know what he was doing and still did not ask him. Sadly he died when only fifty-four. At the time of his death he was a Vice Chairman of GCHQ and a strong candidate for Chairman. For a time he went to Washington where his opposite number was a distinguished American who was made an Honorary KBE and my brother CBE. Again when I met him after my brother's early death, he made no reference to his work, but he did show me his KBE in his study. I remember his wife coming into the room and remarking how unlike him it was to be talking to me about it, to which he replied that it was the first chance he had had. He would not have shown the award to anyone else because they would have asked him how he had got it, which he would not be prepared to tell them

For most of my time I served in three ships – a corvette, a frigate and a sloop – I kept a diary which I still have, recording life in the corvette (*Clematis*) and the frigate (*Exe*). In the sloop, *Amethyst*, I have the records of where we went, but, as the Navigating Officer, there were additional responsibilities and consequently rather less time to keep a diary. I do, however, still have the Navigating Officer's Notebook in which I worked out all the sun and star sights in order to establish our position when we were out of sight of land.

The navigational aids which are used nowadays did not exist then. Consequently every morning at dawn and every evening after sunset

J.R.B.

# UNIVERSITY OF OXFORD

## *JOINT RECRUITING BOARD*

Mr. J.C. Palmer is requested
to present himself for an interview in con-
nexion with his application to the Board
at the University Registry, Old Clarendon
Building, Oxford, at 2.25 p.m. on
Saturday, September 9th 1939.

UNIVERSITY REGISTRY STAMP

All Communications
to be addressed to the
Commanding Officer.
and quote Reference No.

FROM............ THE COMMANDING OFFICER, LONDON DIVISION, R.N.V.R.

H.M.S. PRESIDENT, KING'S REACH, LONDON, E.C. 4.

DATE............ 20th.December,1938.     No. L.D./ N.v. /1938.

TO ...............J.C.Palmer,Esq.,
                 12,Blossom Way,
                 Hillingdon, Mdsx.

SUBJECT........ ENTRY INTO THE R?N.V.R.

FORMER ........

Dear Sir,

          In reply to your letter dated 20th.December,
1938, it is regretted that there are no vacancies for
commissions in the London Division of the R.N.V.R.    I
would point out that direct entry into the Executive
Branch has now ceased, vacancies being filled by suitable
candidates selected from those serving on the lower deck.

          Recruiting for the lower deck is now temporarily
suspended but your name can be noted for entry when enrolment
is resumed, if you so desire.

                    Yours faithfully,

                    Lieut-Commander,R.N.
                    for Commanding Officer.

when the weather permitted, half an hour or so was spent taking sights which then had to be worked out. But it had its compensations. You were not involved in as much watchkeeping as other officers. In my case I just kept the afternoon watch, with, I remember, the Chief Gunner's Mate who was a delightful and extremely efficient Chief Petty Officer with whom I kept in touch for some years after the war. The Captain at that time, quite rightly, thought it important that there should be someone on watch who knew about gunnery which certainly I did not. I had not experienced the rigours of the gunnery school at Whale Island. I remember well that in the evening after taking sights I would be found on the bunk in the Chart House, drinking an excellent mug of cocoa (known as 'Ky') with a book, so that there were peaceful moments even at the worst of times.

Re-reading now what I have recorded in those diaries which I kept, I am struck by how remarkably lucky I was not just to have survived but to have had the chance to serve in the Navy. In a small ship you soon knew the qualities and failings of your shipmates as they did yours. Looking back fifty years later, I realize that qualities then were taken for granted. Only now, for instance, do I appreciate the enormous responsibility that the Captain of a ship took for weeks on end with only a few days in harbour before sailing again to escort another convoy, particularly at a time when the losses were enormous.

When in *Exe* we took part in Operation Torch in North Africa. I am struck by my generally relaxed feelings about it all, as my diary discloses. Yet the risks were of course immense. The voyage out there in the Atlantic and then through the Straits of Gibraltar had all the makings of disaster and yet we made it with comparatively few losses. Having said that and having been there, I confess I do remember, for almost the only time in my five years at sea, feeling it could be the end. The approaches to the Straits had become something of a battleground where many lost their lives. We used to get reports of a number of U-boats round us. It did not incidentally occur to me to wonder how the powers that be ashore knew about the U-boats and certainly not that the reports were the result of the breaking of codes with which my brother was involved. Nothing could have been more depressing than to come upon the bodies of those who had drowned and empty lifeboats. Seldom, I am afraid, did we manage to rescue all of those for whom we looked.

The success of the operation deserved greater praise than perhaps it was accorded at the time. There is reference to those two ships, *Walney* and *Hartland*, and the part which they played. Nothing could have been more courageous. By comparison our patrol, to which there is also reference, was on a different scale of courage, important though it was. The net result of the whole operation was vitally important. It achieved what was planned and the losses were no doubt less than the more pessimistic forecasts. But when you look back now I realize that the dangers were a good deal greater than we appreciated. A member of the ship's company with whom I am still in touch sent me a copy of a letter which he had had from a colleague of his with whom he had served and who had been there in the early days. My friend had asked him whether he remembered many who had been in the ship at that time. His reply might perhaps be regarded as flattering where he said that, of the officers, he remembered best John Palmer, who was the most relaxed member of the ship's company. Little did he know the truth.

There were no covered bridges in those days. In earlier days in *Clematis* it was a distinctly tough life in a small escort ship on the Northern route, past Iceland and Greenland on the way to Newfoundland when spray froze in the rigging and on deck. As much as posssible, I remember, had to be removed to avoid the ship becoming top-heavy. The same applied to *Exe* but not quite so badly, being a bigger ship. But few would have swapped for a less demanding life

My first ship, *Clematis,* was a sister ship of a corvette in which Nicholas Monsarrat served. We were friends and spent many hours together in harbour between convoys mostly in the North Atlantic. I remember him saying he would write about it one day. He knew the life and what was involved. He persuaded me to buy one of his earlier books, *This is the Schoolroom*, which he autographed, saying that one day he would write a best seller which of course he certainly did in *The Cruel Sea*. It is a fair reflection of what life could be like.

*Exe* was a frigate, both an anti-submarine escort and a minesweeper which, like *Amethyst*, was involved both in the Atlantic and the Mediterranean. As during my time in *Clematis*, I kept a surprisingly comprehensive diary. One would be excused for concluding that I must have had plenty of spare time to write a diary. In fact such time as I had was instead of spending it sleeping. Perhaps, at least in rough weather, there was some excuse for illegible writing which certainly has often been very difficult to decipher. Some which can be deciphered I have quoted later.

*Amethyst* was the sloop which made her name up the Yangtse. She had much the greatest armament as well as being the biggest of the three and, incidentally, the most comfortable in which to serve. But there can have been no comfort up the Yangtse. I remain full of admiration for the courage of those concerned and am proud to have the opportunity to meet those who survived at an Annual Reunion.

But before my time in those ships there were three months in merchant ships as a Midshipman, when I also kept a diary. Following a short apprenticeship as a Boarding Officer at Southend, each of us twelve Midshipmen served as what might I suppose in Army terms be described as very junior ADCs to very senior retired Naval Officers, usually Admirals. Their job was Commodore of a convoy in the Atlantic. Their remarkable part in the war has not been adequately acknowledged. They were all over fifty and many over sixty. Half of them were lost. The losses of the merchant ships were appalling. The diary which follows I kept in merchant ships. I was surprised to find I had kept a record of those early days including a visit to my old college at Oxford. I am conscious that the diary clearly reflects that it was written by someone very young and inexperienced.

# CHAPTER II

# Serving with Commodores of Convoys

Sailing with three Commodores (for there were three with whom I served) was, on reflection now some sixty years later, a valuable introduction to life at sea as I was to know it. The war at sea had certainly started. Our losses in those convoys then were a sad introduction to what was to follow. Little did I know what the future would bring. The diary must be read as that of a totally inexperienced boy of nineteen who knew nothing of what life would be like.

There follow pages from my diary at that time.

26 January 1940 – Have spent my last few days ashore in England for some time now. They were good days too : the visit to Oxford – seeing John again: the tea with Roy: the service in chapel with a sermon from the Canon of Liverpool: the dinner in Hall, sitting beside the Abe [in fact the Principal of the College whose name was A.B. Emden] and then to coffee with him afterwards until 9.30. Certainly it all reminded me very vividly of my two years up there but strangely – or perhaps not – I didn't feel in the least bit as if I would really like to go back there. I would go back if it were necessary in order to get a better degree or a qualification for a good job but wrongly, no doubt, I would regard it as a retrograde step. At least this new Naval life does seem to be an advance in that it is something new.

And then the peaceful evening with John by the fire in his room – eating cake and drinking sherry, just like the old days. I shall not easily forget it.

Nor shall I forget the next day at home with M and D – like so many others, perfect. After, as usual, a peaceful and delightful visit to Hillingdon with M and D, over to see my brother Peter. It was very pleasant and pleasing to see him settled so happily in Bush Cottage. It is pretty too: just the sort of place that I have always dreamt of having. I wonder if I ever shall? For some reason I feel I shan't; I always have felt the same. We shall soon see. Let me pray I am wrong.

Now there are other things to think about. Now one's main thoughts will inevitably be centred round such things as Gibraltar, the sea, U-boats, escorts etc. I think, though, that I am in, with the usual luck, for a really pleasant trip. The Commodore, Captain Maundrell, is a most charming man and the Captain of the ship and other officers are equally pleasant. There is certainly rather a shortage of sleeping accommodation but it looks as if it could be quite reasonably comfortable.

Now for a peaceful evening reading and listening to the wireless and, I hope, early to bed. Tomorrow night perhaps there will be rather more for me to write.

**Before sailing we would have had the usual conference at which the Commodore would have told the Captains of all the ships involved what his plans would be in the event of an attack. Unless the signal telling them to scatter were made (which it would be if there were an attack by a capital ship) it would be essential that they retained their stations in the convoy which might well result in having to ignore the sinking of others. It does not need much imagination to realize what life was like in those circumstances.**

27 January 1940 – A miserable day but not badly spent except that I don't have the feeling that we are getting nearer to Gibraltar. Perhaps we aren't yet. As usual have spent the whole day on the bridge and am now trying to manoeuvre for a reasonably comfortable night. It may seem a little better in the morning perhaps. Then we should be collecting more of the convoy coming to join us from Portsmouth. Now for a final visit to the bridge and then, I hope, a few hours in bed.

28 January 1940 – We have lost three of our ships already: seem likely to lose many more, and have so far not yet joined up with the Portsmouth section. And I don't seem to have got very much to say. It's a queer thing. Let us pray the mist will have cleared by the morning. Then across to Ushant?

29 January 1940 – 11.30 am Miserable weather and pitching badly. Speed only four knots. Good night. Apparently we shall be about seven days getting to Gibraltar.

9

<u>7.30 pm</u> We haven't met them yet: hoping to do so tomorrow morning now. In the meantime we continue to roll about in this strong gale. It doesn't seem to affect us in the least though. Every time I look at it I imagine myself sailing *Nomad* out there in these wild seas – probably unable to keep afloat for more than hour at the most – and then I look at all those old merchant ships, just plunging through it. The scene doesn't seem to change at all. I go up at four and see wild seas and eight ships astern with an escort ahead. I go up at six and there are still wild seas and, I hope, eight ships astern – but I can't see them.

<u>29 January 1940</u> – <u>9 pm</u> Have just been up for ten minutes again for a spot of fresh air – and, by Jove, I got it. Wind now appears to have increased, almost dead on port beam, accompanied by heavy rain. Can't believe that we shall ever meet at rendezvous in the morning.

<u>30 January 1940</u> – An exciting day. At 11 am I was wandering peacefully round the deck, looking forward to the usual cup of coffee and deliberating whether I should go below for it or not. At 11.10 am I was drinking an excellent cup of coffee but had only got half through it when at 11.11 am there was a terrific explosion. It conveyed nothing to me though. I heard someone say, 'What in the hell is that' and then, after the first thirty seconds it struck everyone simultaneously to look astern. There on the starboard quarter was some unfortunate ship – afterwards discovered to be the Greek – already well down in the water, hit right amidships. But no more was thought of him. For the next half hour we zigzagged in every imaginable direction at our utmost speed, 12½ although our stated speed is only eleven, whilst the escort disappeared into the mist to deal with the U-boat. It had certainly chosen its time amazingly well and must have been hanging on our tail the whole way. For only ten minutes after the explosion the Greek and all the others were blotted out. It was certainly none too pleasant. There we were charging along in the mist, hoisting one signal after another, hearing gunfire and perhaps depth charges. Fortunately though there were not apparently two of them. But I shall never be able to describe that scene properly. Nor, I fear, will numerous of the unfortunate crew of the Greek. But now we are still in an unpleasant position. The escort of the French section has either left or lost us, leaving only a small trawler, and we have a cheerful report of a U-boat almost in our line. What is more it's a clear night. I'm afraid it won't stop me from sleeping, however, in spite of the

Chief's gruesome story at dinner this evening. An interesting chat with the Mate, too. He obviously feels pretty strongly about the Germans. So do I now!

9.30 pm – Captain again insists that the *Vaclite* was sunk during the night. Everyone, except me, certainly heard loud explosion and now it appears that red flares were seen. That's two out of ten. I wonder how many more there will be.

**The following extract from *The Times* dated 1 February confirms the sinking of *Vaclite*:**

31.January 1940 – 1.30 pm Watching for the blasted U-boats now – infernally tiring too.

7.30 pm – Yet it was, in fact, a most enjoyable afternoon in a way. I thought I should find it excessively tiring but I was so excited by the perfect weather that I forgot all about time. For it really was a remarkable change and I shall not forget the scene as I stood behind that canvas dodger which I had taken the precaution of erecting, in the Bay of Biscay, thinking all the time what a shame it was that I hadn't got a camera. Yet the camera could not have got the atmosphere at all. For it was an entirely strange atmosphere: beauty, hiding a periscope.

Now it is a cloudless sky and visibility must be about two miles at least. We can only pray that no one has seen us, that is all. But I just feel now that I really don't care, so long as it doesn't happen when I am in my pyjamas in bed. I am determined though to change into pyjamas and have a decent night's sleep whatever happens. There is so much that I am conscious of the whole time and so little of it do I remember to put down here.

**My diary entry about *Vaclite* and the article in *The Times* are strange. In fact I remember vividly still, seeing her sunk ahead of us. She was the first ship I had seen sunk and shall not forget it – and yet my diary is different.**

1 February 1940 – 1.30 pm Perfect day again today. News of the *Vaclite*. She was torpedoed. Apparently BBC distorted it though as, no doubt, usual. Interesting really to have a piece of front page news first hand. Glad I wasn't actually in it though. Should like to take a

# ANOTHER U-BOAT SUNK

## BRITISH SHIP LOST IN CONVOY

### RESCUES BY ITALIAN STEAMER

The Admiralty and Air Ministry announce that a U-boat attacked a convoy on the morning of January 30, and sank the British ss. Vaclite, of 5,026 tons, whose crew were rescued by an Italian ship.

The naval escort immediately hunted the submarine and counter-attacked with depth charges, but after a time contact was lost.

Later in the day a flying-boat of the coastal command joined the naval escort to the convoy in the search, and through a gap in the clouds found the submarine, which was proceeding on the surface. It was apparently unable to dive as a result of the damage inflicted during the earlier attack. A heavy bomb was dropped on the starboard side of the submarine. Men were observed on deck and the submarine opened fire with its anti-aircraft gun, the aircraft retaliating with machine-gun fire.

Cloud was now down to sea level, and temporarily obscured the submarine. The aircraft thereupon proceeded to the warships and informed them of the position of the submarine, but when they arrived the submarine had sunk. Some survivors were sighted in a rubber dinghy and were rescued, and some additional survivors were picked up later from the sea by British warships.

The Vaclite was built specially for carrying lubricating oil. She had over 40 separate compartments for holding different grades.

deck chair and book now but instead shall have to go and look for U-boats. Beginning to hope I shall see one!

7.30 pm – Another day nearly over and again I certainly feel like it. Still obviously considerable anxiety about U-boats – and justifiably. After all we've only got this one small trawler as escort.

2 February 1940 – 7.30 pm Sighted one British Light Cruiser and the merchant ships, many seagulls and the usual quota of Chinamen – still many new faces – but otherwise nothing but windy water and overcast sky. In fact today has not been eventful – so far at least – in that no more ships have been torpedoed and we continue to log eight knots. The Frenchman is still with us, although once we thought we had lost him permanently. We went down to lunch and came up to find that he had completely disappeared. However he turned up again later and had only been reconnoitring with true French efficiency. Every now and again I look at him through my glasses and try to pick out faces, often wishing that I could somehow jump on board and talk to them all in French. For I would give a lot at the moment to be able to do that again. Whilst looking for U-boats today I tried to imagine myself walking down the road in Paris. I wonder what it looks like now – just the same; or has it changed like so much else? Surely the door still opens when you press the button; surely the lift still works – and stops: surely the key is still in the top right hand drawer – yes, surely it's still all the same.

But now I am sitting in the Captain's cabin of this tanker, rolling along in convoy down the coast of Portugal about seven days out from London and two from Gibraltar. I wonder where I shall be this time next year?

9.00 pm – It seems an incredibly mild night. Have just been up for ten minutes or so and began to imagine the whole position far more dangerous than I actually know it to be.

3 February 1940 – 9.00 am. Strong gale now but I'm afraid it didn't stop me from getting another good night's sleep. Beginning to feel I shan't be sorry to see Gibraltar – probably Monday morning – although I'm now beginning to feel almost a part of the ship – and you certainly have to work in harmony with it in this weather.

1.30 pm – It would be perfect if only I could take a deck chair and go to sleep in the sun.

8.00 pm – Feeling extraordinarily tired; yet I have done nothing all day really except stand about. Another ship torpedoed – *Amanistan* – who should have been with us. We passed through that position at four am this morning!

6 February 1940 – Have apparently been rather slack about keeping this lately but the fact is that for the last two days of the passage there was really nothing of interest to write about; and during these last two days there has been so much that I haven't had the time or the energy to write anything. Now, though, I am at last comfortably settled in a comfortable bed which remains on an even keel and am looking forward to a really long night, it being now only 9.30.

**Re-reading that diary now I realize how inexperienced I was, knowing nothing of life in the Navy – or indeed the Merchant Navy. But it was an excellent introduction which served me in good stead in the years to come. As I have said in these diaries, and so often thought, I had a charmed life. But at the time I don't think I really realized it. Of course, while I was writing this diary in the merchant ship, the worst of the war at sea had not then started – bad though it was. Unfortunately, but quite understandably, those who were serving in merchant ships, particularly later when losses were so enormous, tended at times to be critical of the part played by the escorts. We, they said, kept away from the U-boats, stationed as we were a mile or two outside the convoy. I remember that I met an old Army friend shortly after the war, who had been in a convoy which had been attacked, being quite critical of the part we had played simply because on that occasion we had not been sunk ourselves.**

Leaving the ship and the Captain and the others at Gibraltar was almost tragic and I felt that I would like to have stayed with them and gone on to Suez. But it is too pleasant here to wish that now. That is if only people will leave me alone and not imagine that I want to be doing something all the time; fortunately, though, at the moment there is no one else here. I feel sure we may have tomorrow, however.

In the meantime I make plans so far as it is possible – for a visit either to Algeçiras and/or Tangier. In each case there is a snag : in the case of Tangier the boats go at all the wrong times. In the case of

Algeçiras where the boats are quite frequent there is the question of a passport. Apart from all that there are the Naval complications.

However, even if I can't get to any of these places I shall be very happy here, reading in the sun on the roof, walking occasionally, eating and sleeping —- tomorrow I propose to settle the travelling question definitely – let us pray successfully.

7 February 1940 – Unfortunately beginning to feel rather ill. It's a very queer thing. I think it must in some way be a reaction after the voyage – though heaven knows why. But there is one great consolation: I have 'successfully settled the travelling question', having got permission to leave for Tangier on Saturday and return on Monday. The only trouble is that it is rather an expensive business, the fare alone, I think, being over £2. However I think I can just manage it and, presuming I can, I am sure it will be worth it.

Today, otherwise, has been quite uneventful. This morning I went down to the office and discovered that all the men down there, including the Captain, are most extraordinarily charming. I was twice presented with a box of chocolates – one by the Captain – and was provided with coffee and biscuits.

I did go to Tangier, having managed to raise sufficient cash for the fare and a hotel when I got there. The whole visit was a great success. The hotel I chose was excellent. I remember that bed and breakfast was 12/6. I had breakfast on the balcony outside my room. I don't remember dinner so well but one could not have had breakfast in a more lovely setting, nor a better meal. The balcony overlooked the beach. While I was there I saw three Arabs and two camels approaching the town along the beach, no doubt to conduct some of their business, whatever that was, before making their way inland again. It was a scene totally detached from the war. Indeed one had the feeling that they would not even have known that there was a war on. The next morning, after exploring the town which intrigued me, I returned to Gibraltar. All went according to plan except that the unusual motion of the tug very nearly made me sick.

13 February 1940 – Last night here now. I cracked up completely on Thursday afternoon and decided on Friday morning that I would have to stay in bed, which I did, under the care of Surgeon Lieutenant Miller RNVR, until Sunday afternoon, feeling ghastly. A bit better

15

now, though, and should I think be able to survive the trip. Let us pray it will be comfortable! Apparently it will be Liverpool! Am sharing room tonight with RNR Midshipman.

15 February 1940 – 1000 On board the *Waranga* – Came on board after the conference at about 1230, eagerly expecting to find a really comfortable ship with the possibility of a cabin to myself for a change. But most disappointed to find again that they had very little accommodation and that I would have to sleep aft with the cadets. However they are very decent fellows and I have at least got a comfortable bunk to myself. Unfortunately, though, it was decided that I would go on watch and, since they were doing double watches, it means four on and four off which will, eventually, be distinctly tiring for it's impossible to get more that three and a half hours' sleep at a time. But it's another new experience and another very different ship from the last. So is the captain. He's rather a 'pansy' and obviously thinks he should be an admiral, walking about with a white-bound telescope and obviously insisting upon strict discipline. It's extraordinary the way these ships vary. This is quite different from the previous ship where everything was taken so delightfully casually and the officers aren't nearly so pleasant either – anything like.

Still seems a long way to go and we've not done a day of it yet. I wonder what there will be in store for us. But at least we got through the Straits without any incident. Can we get all the way home without an attack?

16 February 1940 – 1.30 pm Inspite of these double watches and the inevitable rather severe lack of sleep, life continues to be quite pleasant and we make unusually good progress in perfectly peaceful weather. If only it would last until we have got clear of the Bay of Biscay, at least, we might make Liverpool even by Thursday evening – which would be perfect.

Now that I have got the camera there are, of course, no photographs to be taken that would be worthwhile for there is no real point in taking anything but a potential picture. With these small negatives it must be a waste of money to enlarge anything else. Last night I slept from 8.30 until 11.30 and then from 4.30 until 7.30, which was not at all bad, but tonight will not be so good. I shall only be able to sleep between twelve and four. So far, however, I don't seem to feel it very badly. Now I will read and sleep until four. Michael

16

Arlen's *Lili Christine*. Mottram's *Early Morning* seemed rotten – not at all like *Spanish Farm*.

<u>7.45 pm</u> Just preparing to go up on watch now. I'm afraid it'll be very dark and cold. Discussions in dinner tonight as to when we should reach Liverpool. The doctor a great character – apparently he once operated for appendicitis in the middle of a gale. Quite a pleasant afternoon – actually did something for a change, taking bearings.

<u>17 February 1940</u> – <u>0905</u> The night over reasonably easily and I didn't have to be up until six this morning. I am beginning to realize, though, more and more what a little even the busiest man does on board a ship. Ninety per cent of his time is spent just standing about and the other ten per cent just doing things which must inevitably after a time become quite mechanical. I don't know whether it's the same in the Navy but if it is – and I imagine it must be – I certainly couldn't stand it as a career.

**I was soon to discover that was not the case.**

**And so I continued to walk up and down the bridge, eat an occasional toffee, an occasional piece of chocolate and every now and again to take a bearing or a sight with the sextant just to ease the monotony. But no one else does much more.**

<u>18 February 1940</u> – <u>1.15 pm</u> Last night at 5.30 a message from leading ship in port column – 'Please pass to Commodore; Fourth Engineer has died of heart failure. Propose dropping out of convoy 11 am tomorrow for burial. Do you agree?' That was all it said and mechanically it was passed to the Commodore. Mechanically he replied 'Regret death : agree.' So at 10.45 this morning, the *Runswick* having dropped out, colours were hoisted at half mast and we steamed mechanically on whilst the poor fellow was buried only four days from England which he probably hadn't seen for two or three months. 'Heart failure' : it is the sort of thing that a Fourth Engineer would die of. Nowhere in a ship could be more dangerous than the engine room in the event of an attack.

Otherwise we continue at a good speed – logging 8½ and some-times nine – in calm weather, still without any incidents. I am getting better and better at getting through the watches without undue

17

impatience, even so I shan't be sorry for a really good bath – even if it does cost 2/6 at the Adelphi – and a long night in pyjamas.

9 February 1940 – 1000 Beginning to get colder now and I put on a jersey for the first time this morning. A fairly strong following wind and sea on the quarter, rolling pleasantly – about half way across the bay. Last night about 10.30 the Commodore's ship started to forge ahead, logging nine knots, with the result that we left the rest of the convoy miles behind. I went down to tell the Commodore who came up ten minutes later – having been asleep – and staggering on to the bridge, giving the false impression that he had had too many whiskies and sodas, exclaimed with considerable irritation, 'It's a bit hazy isn't it?' Actually it was one of the clearest nights we have had.

I have passed the time on watch lately dreaming of our days at Minsmere and on the Broads. The pre-breakfast bathe, breakfast. Then the peaceful visit to Dunwich, eagerly visiting the Post Office to call for letters; another bathe and lunch, followed by an afternoon reading and asleep; then – and this I remember particularly vividly for some reason – tea of bread and jam and excellent cake in rather a hurry, whilst Rip (the dog) stood by miserably, knowing that we were going to play golf and not take him for a walk. I remember the golf so vividly too – every hole and so many incidents. It was a perfect holiday. How I would love to do it all over again. How I would love too to go on the Broads again. I wonder if we ever shall?

I have just finished Michael Arlen's *Lili Christine*. Very third rate, as D would say, I thought. He doesn't seem to have troubled to think it out anything like carefully enough before starting and obviously couldn't decide how to finish it. There's not enough material for anything more than a short story.

21 February 1940 – 1000 Forgot it yesterday. Back in the English climate again now and although the temperature is still fifty degrees I feel colder than I have felt for many weeks. Yesterday we, at last, left the other section of the convoy resulting in two hours of con-tinuous panic from four to six, during which time the poor old Commodore completely lost control. From that moment we returned to the old state of affairs, with him on the bridge all the time with the result that I had to appear at four am lest he should come up. He did. But now I begin to feel distinctly tired. It seems though that we shall certainly be there tomorrow evening. Now for a read and some

sleep to fortify myself before going up on that appallingly draughty bridge.

22 February 1940 – Well here I am in the train to London.

Now for impressions of the voyage; it always seems that my first impressions of these ships are bad but the more I see of the people the more I like them until, at the end of the trip, I am always very sorry to leave. The *Waranga* I was particularly sorry about. I realized how much I had enjoyed myself and what a great affection I had for the ship and the officers. It is a vivid impression which I think I shall never forget, so I need not worry about putting it all down here. I become more and more inclined to think, though, that the Merchant Service would, at the last resort, be a very good job. I remember it so well. I wish I had had a camera to take the old ship.

At that stage of my Naval career leave was generous, not intentionally but there always tended to be an interval between leaving one ship and joining the next.

On the morning before sailing, the Masters of the ships which would be in the convoy were, as I have mentioned earlier, asked to assemble to meet the Commodore who then had the opportunity to tell them how he proposed to manage the convoy and what was expected of them. They were given a plan which they were to follow showing the position of each ship in the convoy. In particular, he told them what action he would take in the event of a serious attack by U-boats or a surface ship. It was then that the order to scatter would be signalled, the object, of course, being to make it more difficult for an attack. But again the risks were immense. Inevitably some ships were attacked and sunk with tragic losses. But at my age, then nineteen, I was ignorant of what to expect. Every month the duties and responsibilities of Commodores were becoming greater. It was then that the lives of so many were being lost, including, in many cases, the Commodores.

24 March 1940 – Left Southend Pier with Admiral Hamilton – usual paraphernalia – at 5.30 for the SS *Karabagh*. I had hoped that, for once, I would be fortunate in getting a really comfortable ship, with a cabin to myself but again, as usual, I found myself on a settee. But how much worse it nearly was!

It was eventually decided that I should have the spare cabin aft to myself. There were vague stories of a few cockroaches but, feeling

19

unusually brave, I swept them aside with 'Oh, I don't mind cock-roaches'. Eventually the time came to see it and certainly there were cockroaches; in a minute I saw half a dozen crawling up the walls. My heart sank appreciably, but still, through sheer stubbornness, I felt sufficiently brave to say, this time 'Oh, that doesn't matter; they won't stop me from sleeping.' But then, an hour later, I returned again – 'Goodnight Mr. Palmer I hope you sleep well'. Immediately I got into the cabin the worst dawned on me. Horror struck, I walked to the bunk and pulled back the clothes. There were three enormous ones. Then I lifted the pillow! It was too much: I confessed to myself that I could not face it. I am now sleeping on the settee in the Third Mate's cabin and have appreciated even more the generosity and good nature of these MN officers.

**I still remember the occasion vividly. It was not the first time I had seen cockroaches nor the last, but I have never since seen anything like it and can, I think, be excused for not feeling able to sleep there.**

25 March 1940 – 1.0 pm Long talk with the mate last night. A lovely fellow who used to be a salesman in a shop.

10 pm – Another chat with the mate; extraordinarily sensitive and appreciative. A long day which slowly got worse, so far as the weather was concerned; now rain and mist but we have joined up all right. It seems I shall have quite an interesting time and, as usual, I find everyone most charming. If only people at home could realize what these chaps go through, how differently they would feel about rationing. It's Easter Monday today; I hadn't realized it. This time last year we were on the Broads. Now I am in this cabin of a merchant ship between Land's End and Finisterre, and there is a war on. Again I ask, where shall I be this time next year?

26 March 1940 – 10.30 pm – Went down into the engine room this evening with mate. It certainly made me admire more and more the way these fellows stick to it.

29 March 1940 – Went on the Third Mate's watch last night and talked solidly the whole time – father originally a grocer; trained as one himself and at age of fourteen won all the prizes. Then on fifteenth birthday saw a lorry going to Swansea and without any

premeditation just got on the back. Shipped as cabin boy in a small Norwegian round to Cardiff, sold papers and ate one pig's trotter in four days and then went home by lorry again. Since then has served five years in the fo'c's'le.

That was my last experience of life in a merchant ship in convoy in those early years. It had all been a great experience which I still remember with a mixture of nostalgia and admiration. The fact is that the country could not have survived without them. When subsequently serving in an escort in the Atlantic I became increasingly conscious of their courage as losses continued to grow.

Before joining a corvette, I was sent to *King Alfred*, the base in Brighton where RNVR officers had a month's training in such basic things as marching. Having been at St. Paul's, where the OTC was not compulsory and I had avoided it, to march in step was something quite new to me and I was no good at it. Indeed my squad was called 'the Awkward Squad' by the instructor with some justification. But it was all good experience. I feel guilty now that I did not volunteer to take a small boat across the channel for the Dunkirk evacuation but there was, a week or so beforehand, no indication of why we were wanted. If I had realized I would certainly have gone. Perhaps it was another example of my good luck, for certainly a few who did volunteer failed to return.

# CHAPTER III

# HMS *Clematis* in the Battle of the Atlantic

*Clematis,* the corvette which I was to join, was one of the early Flower Class corvettes. She was built at Bristol, the first Naval ship to be have been built there for ninety years. It is sad that none of those remarkable little ships has been preserved, for it might well be said that their part in the Battle of the Atlantic was as unique as that of the Spitfires in the Battle of Britain. Nicholas Monsarrat's novel *The Cruel Sea* painted an accurate picture of the part they played and of the lives of those who served in them. To have flown a Spitfire would for us have been quite impossible to contemplate, but perhaps a Spitfire pilot would have said the same of serving in a corvette in the North Atlantic. Yet now, more than fifty years later, the memory of those years is such that only the diary, which I kept intermittently and which I have just re-read for the first time, can recall a life which in truth few of us would have wanted to miss.

I well remember joining *Clematis,* having completed the course at *King Alfred.* I was told to report to Swansea where she was building. I set off to Paddington Station where my parents also came to see me off. Inevitably it must have been a distinctly sad occasion for them. By extraordinary chance we met on the platform one of the Cambridge contingent – John Ellyatt – who was there also with his parents and his sister, Mary, then at school at Sherborne with special leave. We met again later when she was a boating Wren in Plymouth.

Her brother and I duly reported to the Naval authorities at Swansea only to be told that no such ship was there. Finally, after some research, it was established that she was in Bristol. There we found her. She was under the command of an RNR Commander who I noticed had already got a DSO and DSC. The First Lieutenant was an RNR Lieutenant. Otherwise there were just the two RNVR Sub-Lieutenants – my brother-in-law to be and myself. The First Lieutenant to whom I refer later was the officer who was sunk, picked up and then sunk again. He too was a fine seaman.

We were very kindly treated by the builder, Charles Hill, and indeed by everyone in Bristol. I remember particularly the kindness of Charles Hill who invited the officers to lunch the day before we sailed. Harveys (the wine merchants) too were particularly kind and hospitable.

The next day we sailed down the Avon and then round the coast to Scotland.

As we sailed, I was very conscious that we were in the first new ship to do so for ninety years.

Sadly I cannot remember who wrote the ode 'To HMS *Clematis*' which follows.

Re-reading my diaries now, I cannot help being struck by the mixture of all the various actions on the one hand and, on the other, by the philosophical thoughts of a twenty-year-old. Anyone reading them will not, I hope, find the comments too superfluous.

In those days all those who were going to be in involved in escort duties were ordered to Tobermory on the island of Mull to 'work up' as the two or three days there were described. One was under the orders of a great man, Admiral Stephenson, who was superficially exceptionally tough but at heart the kindest of men. We went there in *Clematis* as, later, in my two other ships, *Exe* and *Amethyst*. I remember very well an incident in *Amethyst* when, on a beautiful afternoon when nothing else was on, I decided to go for a sail in the Sound of Mull. I took one of the ship's whalers and two sailors with me. We had a wonderful sail, in ideal conditions. At one stage I noticed a whole lot of flags had been hoisted in *Amethyst*, but since I never mastered flags I took no notice and continued the sail. Finally when I came in and tied up I was immediately shown to my horror the Admiral's barge coming out towards us. There was no officer of the watch available. I realized that I would have to receive the Commodore myself, dressed in an old pair of shorts and a pretty dirty shirt. When he came on board, he said ' Did you not know that you are not allowed to sail in the Sound and did you not see flags on your ship recalling you?' 'No sir,' I replied, 'I did not see anything', which on the spur of the moment seemed the safest answer. He then lectured me pretty fiercely, looked around the ship, finally turning to me before leaving and saying, 'I am sure you had a good sail and enjoyed it'. That was typical of him.

Having completed the three-day 'work up', the first entry in my *Clematis* diary, when we were sailing to pick up our first convoy, reads;-

We left at 0700, wind freshening from the North West. It didn't look healthy – visibility was poor and low cloud was making the

23

# To H.M.S. Clematis

Hail Clematis! Thou wert not born in lady's bower
Thou'rt sterner stuff, though still the Flower of Chivalry.
To keep the freedom of the seas for those
Who take their business to the sea in ships—
Protecting, succouring and befriending them through all:
A very Flower of Chivalry!

Hail Clematis! Born in a city of the West
Where " ship-shape, Bristol fashion" was our boast of old
And still is!—Go thou forth to conquer evil things
To slay, exterminate and crush beyond uprise
All that is wrong and holding souls of men in bond.
We hail thee Clematis! The Flower of Chivalry.

M.B.D.

12th July, 1940.

west coast look as sinister as it can look beautiful. It wasn't healthy. By 0930 I had been sick – so had nearly everyone else – and by 1030 there were six inches of fuel oil and water in the wardroom and in my cabin. It got worse steadily. By lunch time no one was really capable. Life seemed hardly worth living, I remember. That night, or rather the next morning, when I was keeping the morning watch, was the worst I can remember. I could hardly stand. Waves broke green over the open bridge and she was rolling so far that the boats touched the water on either side. 'Ship shape and Bristol fashion'. Certainly she seemed she must be to survive such conditions.

It was as well I did not realize how much worse conditions would often be but by then we had got used to it. Two days later I wrote:- 'Now we have broken down and are alone stopped and a sitting target while the Engineer struggles to cure the problem.' He did after three hours.

It was not long after that when one of the ships in the convoy broke down and we took it in tow – a fairly hazardous operation. Again it was typical of Commander Cleeves to embark on it. I think the idea of salvaging a ship appealed to him in spite of offers from others to take over the tow. We took her back to the west coast of Scotland. It was a very pleasant surprise when some three months later we all had a share of the salvage that was payable. I do remember that my share was five pounds.

While we never had to escort one of the Russian convoys, we had plenty of cold weather south of Iceland and Greenland when on our way to Newfoundland. Indeed the weather could not have been much worse with the rigging and deck frozen with ice which we had to do our best to get rid of to avoid becoming too top heavy. At least the Admiralty were good enough to supply us with gear designed to protect those engaged in the convoys from excessive cold. An open bridge in a gale and below zero temperatures was not a place one would choose at four o'clock in the morning. Indeed with hindsight one does wonder how the crews of those ships survived.

One place in Newfoundland to which we went was Placentia Bay. It had been the meeting place for Winston Churchill and President Roosevelt not long before. One afternooon while we were there, waiting for the next homeward bound convoy, I was able to get ashore. I walked to a sheep station some five miles inland which I enjoyed, not least because I was able to buy an excellent sheepskin-lined coat which I remember wearing on the way home with the convoy and which subsequently I gave to my wife to be.

25

While at Placentia Bay Petty Officer Sewell and Acting Petty Officer Commons both got into trouble for drinking too much and causing a disturbance ashore. Cleeves asked me to represent them in the Police Court which I must say was a novel experience for me. Little did I know then that five or six years later, when qualified as a solicitor, I would quite often find myself defending in similar circumstances.

There follows my report to the Captain of the ship. I was relieved that all went well. Certainly the magistrate was very understanding when he said what he did in dismissing the case.

Needless to say, Sewell and Commons were first-class seamen. It is not perhaps generally publicized enough that the Navy was at that time very dependent on the Petty Officers and Chief Petty Officers who knew much more about the sea than us amateurs. In a corvette you would have two or three Chief Petty Officers. I am sure it is no exaggeration to record that without them corvettes, in particular, would have found life extremely difficult. As an example, when we sailed in *Clematis* leaving the dock in Bristol and down the Avon, I was in theory in charge aft. An order came down to get out a spring. Extraordinarily, I had absolutely no idea what the order meant and simply turned to one of the Petty Officers. I told him to get out a spring and was intrigued to watch what happened.

It is interesting to recall what was involved in escorting a convoy in those days. While the convoy, under command of the Commodore, zigzagged, the escorts were bound to do the same. It was not difficult in the dark to lose the convoy, which occasionally one did. Making contact with it again on a wild night or sometimes in fog was not easy. It is difficult now to imagine quite what life was like when surrounded by U-boats as all too often one was and to picture the sight of a ship being sunk while we tried desperately to get the U-boat responsible. You needed considerable determination and courage for an escort to continue to do its best to escort the remaining ships while knowing of all the survivors who stood little chance of being saved. Looking back now, it feels like the most appalling nightmare, but it was true.

A convoy which we escorted in the North Atlantic and of which details are available from German records is fairly typical of what tended to be the same for other convoys on that route. It was, for instance, on that route that escorting the convoy of fifty-two ships thirty-seven were lost. The one referred to by German records was between 19 October and 30 October 1941, when, en route from Europe again to Newfoundland, on the first day at sea German records show that *U84* sighted the convoy and attacked unsuccessfully. The following day, however, *U123*

HMS CLEMATIS
April 22nd 1942.

Sir,

I have the honour to submit the following report of proceedings at the Placentia Police Court at 11.5 April 20th.
Petty Officer James SEWELL and Acting Petty Officer John COMMONS appeared before the court charged with —:

        (i) Being drunk
        (ii) Behaving in a disorderly manner

in the Main Street of Placentia at approximately 1800 April 19th. A charge of obstructing the Police Constable in the execution of his duty was withdrawn.

Evidence was later given in court and I did not see the Police Constable who made the arrest but I understood from the Sergeant that it was

more for their own safety than through the necessity
of preserving good order that they had been
arrested.        The second charge of behaving
in a disorderly manner was not stressed.
On being asked by the Magistrate in the court
whether I wished to move any motion I said
that both Petty Officers had excellent records in
the ship and requested that if possible they
might be released into Naval custody
I said I was sure they were both regretted
what had happened.
In releasing them the Magistrate said he
did not consider the case at all serious so
far as Naval Authorities were concerned

            I am, Sir,
            Your obedient Servant

            Holmes.   Lieut R.N.V.R
                            —

torpedoed the Armed Merchant Cruiser *Ausonia*. That evening *U123* directed *U203* and *U82* to the convoy and *U82* sank two ships, totalling 9317 tons. The following day, 22 October, when the convoy was escorted by the sloops *Wellington* and *Stork*, by the destroyer *Beverley* and by the corvettes *Clematis* and *Asphodel*, German reconnaissance sighted us, but the attack from *U85*, *U202* and *U203* were successfully driven off on 23 October. Following that encounter, the U-boat route was, according to German records, sent again to its Central Atlantic patrol line. In addition *U123* was sent to Belle Isle Strait off Nova Scotia.

Certainly such attacks were fairly typical of what happened frequently in those waters and resulted in heavy losses. It was then that Churchill concluded that the Battle of the Atlantic was vital and indeed it was soon after that he persuaded Roosevelt to let the British Navy have some of the American destroyers. Unsatisfactory ships though they were with their four funnels, they were nevertheless very valuable as were any other steps that could be taken to defeat U-boats in the Atlantic.

The most unusual action for *Clematis* was on Christmas Day 1940. At seven o'clock in the morning the Officer of the Watch heard what he thought was thunder but a moment later realized it was not when shells dropped round the ship and flashes were seen on the horizon. Action stations were sounded. The Captain was quickly on the bridge and had no doubt what should be done. He altered course towards the battleship which was then visible and made an open signal to the Admiralty, 'Am engaging unknown enemy battleship' and gave our position. Having opened fire, he then ordered smoke to be made to conceal the convoy. Commander Cleeves was a remarkable character. He had already got his DSO and a DSC in Norway. Later there is reference to his memorial service. I decided that he was now after a VC which inevitably would be a posthumous one. By then we were some three to four miles from the German ship. It would clearly be a hopeless battle with our one four-inch gun against the battleship's enormous armament. On our port quarter the troop-carrying ship, *Empire Trooper*, was in great danger, having been hit twice. Fortunately three light cruisers of ours, which were round the other side of the convoy, now appeared – *Berwick*, *Bonaventure* and *Dunedin*. *Berwick*, which was the first to appear, opened fire but of course neither she, nor all three of them, was any match for what we later knew was the *Hipper*. The future at that moment looked very bleak, not just for us but also for the three light cruisers and the convoy, to which the Commodore had made a signal to scatter. I remember my future brother-in-law saying, 'In a minute we shall have our heads blown off'.

It had certainly been a memorable sight to see *Bonaventure* pulling out with us, drawing ahead to engage the raider whilst we and *Dunedin* laid a smoke screen. But it was misty, the convoy scattered and the German got away. We were soon on our own, ploughing through more heavy weather.

Most fortunately, however, German records now show that the Captain of the *Hipper*, who was at the start of an Atlantic cruise with orders to sink any of our ships he could find, decided that he did not want to become involved in a battle so soon. *Berwick* had been hit, but so also, although not causing any appreciable damage, had the *Hipper*. We lived to fight another day. It was then that one of the ship's company wrote the verse which follows.

> Twas Xmas day on the *Clematis,*
> The roughest day of the year
> When up spoke the starboard lookout
> "Blimey, the *Admiral Scheer*!"
>
> Then action stations sounded,
> The Action Bell was rung,
> And up dashed Buffs and four seamen
> To fire the four inch gun.
>
> This Christmas morning action
> Was causing quite a stir,
> What are those flashes Yeoman?
> "I think it's lightning sir."
>
> Then salvoes started falling
> With a very angry tone,
> "Let her have it " yelled a seaman,
> As he rammed the H.E. home.
>
> The sparkers in the office,
> Both Moggs and Matt were there
> "Report the enemy" yelled Yorkie,
> The sparkers answered" Where?"
>
> Full ahead on the engine,
> All sixteen knots flat out,
> To make smoke around the convoy
> And it smoked the stokers out

Corvettes close for action
And the rain began to clear,
Twas there they saw the target,
German Battleship, maybe the *Scheer*.

The battle went on raging
The hotter flew the fray
A time we will all remember
1940 – Xmas Day.

The corvette charged their target,
The enemy withdrew,
When up came *Berwick, Bonaventure* and *Dunedin*,
Three bolts from the blue

There came the Xmas dinner,
It made the lads see red
Plum duff, big eats and turkey!
No, more corned beef and bread.

Messes are underwater.
And all our clothes are wet,
But are we yet downhearted,
*Clematis*, no, not yet!

Commander Cleeves sent the following signal to the Admiralty and at the same time circulated his congratulations to the ship's company:

> Engaged unknown enemy raider. *Empire Trooper* hit, damage believed slight. Convoy scattered under Commodore's order. *Bonaventure* and *Dunedin* pursuing.
>
> I would like to congratulate everyone on their part yesterday. We shall not forget Xmas 1940.

The First Lord of the Admiralty at that time was A.V. Alexander. He made reports to the House of Commons every month of Naval activity. Some two months after the *Hipper* incident he told the House that the report he had received of a corvette opening fire and engaging what she had reported as 'an unknown enemy battleship' had brought 'tears to his eyes'. Later the Weekly Intelligence Reports also reported the incident, a copy of which follows:-

31

At 0930 Dec.25 H.M.Corvette *Clematis*, one of the escorts of a convoy, reported that she was engaging an unknown enemy raider in a position 700' west of Cape Finisterre 43 22 : 25 20, that one of the connvoy had been slightly damaged and that H.M.Ships *Berwick* and *Bonaventure* were in chase. The convoy was scattered. At 0942 *Berwick* reported that she had sighted an enemy capital ship (Deutschland class) twelve miles to the westward, steering on a W'y course. The description of the raider was afterwards corrected to an 8" cruiser. H.M.Ships *Berwick* and *Bonaventure* engaged to drive off the enemy but lost sight of him at 1056 owing to the poor visibility. The chase was abandoned at 1125. *Berwick* was slightly damaged in the engagement. She reported that she made one hit on the enemy above the funnel and possibly other hits. At about noon on the 28th *Bonaventure* intercepted the German *Boden*, 8,200 tons about 70 miles north-east of the position of the action with the raider and sunk her by torpedo as the weather was unsuitable for boarding. By Dec 30 all ships of the convoy had been collected and it is now known that a second ship was also slightly damaged by the raider's attack.

Reading my diary again now, which I have not looked at for at least sixty years, it is clear that *Clematis* must surely have had a charmed life. With hindsight, it becomes more and more clear to me that we were enormously lucky not to have been hit by one of the shells which hit the *Empire Trooper*, quite apart from the many chances of being sunk by a U-boat. And then later, when escorting the convoy south from Gibraltar, considerable risks were again taken. No doubt it is always the case, whether in the Army or the RAF, that only years later, when reminded of what you were doing, do you appreciate how fortunate you were and how tragic was the fate of those who were sunk with little hope of rescue.

I wrote later in my diary:

It seems to be very trite, just like one long dream, this trip. I had hardly had time to relax from the enormous reactions of leave before, the next day (18th), we sailed from Liverpool. It was then, and still is, impossible to realize that we may be away from England until the war is over; impossible to realize that perhaps next time I go home the windows will be unblacked —- the French windows will be open, the light shining across the lawn to the green gate.

But I remembered such things as that in an amazingly vivid way at 7.30 last Wednesday morning when shells were dropping all round us – and unpleasantly alone. That certainly was a nightmare; we felt so helpless, expecting every moment, with horribly vivid imagination, to have (as Ellyatt said) 'one's head blown off'. Most clearly was the necessity for having some particular job to do demonstrated. I noticed it in myself, and I noticed many obviously running around quite aimlessly, trying to find some job to keep them occupied. It was all over quite soon. We were the first to open fire and managed to get five rounds in before *Bonaventure* had pulled out from the convoy, by which time the *Trooper* had been hit.

It is an understatement to say we were fortunate to have survived as were *Berwick, Bonaventure* and *Dunedin*. It is clear now from German records that it was the decision of the Captain of the *Hipper* not to continue the action so early in their cruise looking for trouble in the Atlantic which saved us from what would have been for us an inevitably diastrous action and no doubt also saved many of the merchant ships. We had instructions to proceed to the Azores and then to escort the *Empire Trooper* to Gibraltar.

Ponta Delgarda was amusing; arrived there at midnight. We waited to enter until daylight. At seven we thought we had been fired on but we later discovered it to be a U-boat within the three-mile limit which was attacking an unfortunate Panamanian ship – a pity we didn't know. But soon we had for us a unique experience in that quaint harbour when a Portuguese destroyer offcer called on us with all the pomp and ceremony of peacetime, in cocked hat and sword, to find our wardroom six inches deep in water, pineapples, oranges, bananas and chickens – not to mention members of the English colony of eighteen, totally cut off since the beginning of the war, except for a few ships like ourselves. We left soon afterwards to escort the *Empire Trooper* to Gib. As we were leaving, I noticed the Captain looking back at the lights. It was something, of course, which we had not seen since the beginning of the war.

1 January 1941 – I heard Big Ben strike whilst I was on watch last night. It was ten by our time, when quite unexpectedly I heard it. The WT office had switched on the loudspeaker, so that even standing on the bridge I could hear it clearly. Two years ago I remember we were all home. We strolled out on the lawn to hear the bells ringing at Hillingdon Church. We felt quite emotional even then – what must

33

we feel now? I would feel less, I fear, for this last year has exhausted all that, leaving an old record on which the needle gets stuck in the same groove, playing over and over again – until through sheer lack of power it runs down – 'When will it be over?' And when I wind it up again and shift the needle from the groove, it merely gets stuck in the next one – 'Will it ever be over, will it ever be over?' But what can one say on New Year's Day – or think – that is not conventional? As the look-out said to me, 'I wonder what this year will bring us, Sir?' That is what we are all thinking today – whether we admit it or not – 'Where shall I be this time next year?'

2 January 1941 – An uneventful day during which the old *Trooper* has caused much aggravation by her slowness. In fact I was told that for'ard there is a rumour that he – the captain – is fifth column. At least they might be fair and accuse the Chief Engineer. Talked to the coxswain of the news and other things – Japan says she doesn't want war with anyone and Hitler says that God is on his side. The coxswain talked of medals and decorations and said with some feeling that he is not interested in medals – all he wants is his life. He said the usual things too, of course, about medals being given to the wrong people, or at least missing so many who deserve them. Stannard VC has been mentioned in despatches. His ship was sunk off Cape Wrath. Of course he deserved his VC and other decorations but there must be so many others who have been overlooked. That is inevitable. We should make Gib by Sunday anyhow.

3 January 1941 – 'Dublin bombed'. It seems good news (if it is true; we get so many rumours here). Yet surely it must have been a mistake? The last thing Hitler can want is to bring Eire into the war and he must realize that invasion would be bound to fail – it would be even more difficult than England itself. At least it may have woken the Irish up a bit too – it is high time they did something. We still plug on with *Empire Trooper*. I was rather caught napping by *Kenya* tonight. Feeling most disillusioned about the weather, unusually calm for Gib, I was not keeping as efficient a look out as I should. Suddenly I heard a humming noise on our beam and found it to be *Kenya* who was challenging us, and probably had been doing so for many minutes – 'You should keep a better look out.' — It is hard to say it but I hope Dublin will be bombed again – just enough to wake them up.

<u>4 January 1941</u> – Still ploughing on.

<u>5 January 1941</u> – Arrived at last, thank God.

**Certainly I do remember a strong feeling of relief after that distinctly hazardous trip.**

**By chance it was then that I saw an article in the *Daily Herald*, a well known paper in those days. It records very fairly the part played by corvettes at that time. A copy of the article follows:**

## CORVETTES ARE SAVING CONVOYS

British merchant shipping losses have been getting smaller. Why? The corvette, Britain's new type of warship, now being built on mass production lines, is part of the answer. Here A.J. McWhinnie, *Daily Herald* Naval Correspondent, tells you about life in these tiny saviours of the convoys.

'The Atlantic outlook is brightening.

For a fortnight I have been sailing thousands of miles out there, investigating the dangers, assessing the possibilities for the immediate future, and observing changes and developments in our unceasing fight against the U-boats across the biggest battlefront of all.

Things have been moving rapidly since my last Atlantic trip with a destroyer in December.

Outstanding are these facts, gathered with our Northern patrols and later with the vital convoys from the Americas.

British escort forces out there today are steadily being strengthened.

Ships may still be torpedoed at times. But the chances of convoys getting through are better than they were at the beginning of the winter.

There are several developments which, if even hinted at, would be of vital value to the enemy.

The ships of this particular convoy had their holds stacked with foodstuffs and war supplies and planes from America.

*Not a ship was lost throughout the run. But there is a crippled U-boat out there somewhere. A corvette did that – one of the toughest little warships in the world.*

I am the first Naval correspondent to sail in these new anti-submarine ships, testing their endurance and fighting efficiency in northern blizzards, howling gales, and head-on to the Atlantic rollers.

These long-funnelled, whale-catcher type of warships, smaller than destroyers, were the answer to Britain's prayer when the Atlantic outlook was blackest, when France had caved in and we had to fight alone.

There was no time to build destroyers to beat the new intensive U-boat Blitz. So crisis decisions were taken.

Many slipways must be used to rush out corvettes. Organization between builders and sub-contractors must be such that mass production methods could be used. Corvettes must be rushed out to sea on chain-belt principles. And today you find corvette groups operating alongside the destroyers and sloops with the convoys.

Their advantages are these:-

(1) They can fight U-boats in the foulest weather.

(2) They can be built reasonably quickly – I look forward to the time when, from a single slipway, one corvette can be put to sea every month.

(3) A corvette costs only a fraction of the cost of a destroyer. Numbers count in screening a convoy from U-boats, so that cost of escort craft comes down.

(4) The range of these tiny warships is a secret, but they are fitted with the same efficient anti-submarine gear as the crack destroyers. And submarine protection has been recently further improved.

(5) While not so fast as destroyers, they are fast enough to pursue the U-boats, and that's all the speed they need for the job for which they are being built.

(6) They need only fifty men – a third of a ship's company of a destroyer.

(7) A corvette is in herself only a tiny target, whether she is being attacked from the air or on, or under, the sea.

I see no reason why we should not have two or three hundreds of these corvette anti-submarine warships sooner than most people might think. That number would be a first class insurance against U-boats.

They are lively in a seaway. The men who sail in them suffer discomfort in even the slightest swell. And when they are battling through the winter gales, their broad beams roll with the sickening movement of a fat goldfish flicking its tail to jerk over on its side when somebody bangs its bowl.

I have sailed more than 25,000 miles covering the war at sea, mainly in destroyers, but I've never known anything like the roll you get in these corvettes.

The corvette men have been hand-picked for their endurance. And when they prove they can take it, they say they wouldn't change. They are proud of their task.

They had to be on this trip, what with gales and blizzards, squalls and storms, and three days living on hard tack.

They certainly earn their 'hard-lying money.' Outside the submarine there isn't a tougher job afloat.

Commanding officer of the corvette in which I sailed is an RN commander who likes being a small ship man while his son is in the biggest warship of all – the *Hood*.

The first lieutenant was a luxury liner officer in peacetime. He was RNR and found himself in the doomed armed merchant cruiser *Patroclus*. He clung to a tiny raft for seven and a half hours before a destroyer picked him up.

The navigator has been seven times round the world in tramp ships. He is only twenty-seven now. The sub-lieutenant (RNVR) is a 21-year-old baronet.

Down on the mess deck they yarn about their adventures earlier in the war. Most of them have been 'over the side.' Most of them have had their baptism of fire at sea.

I'd back these corvette men in a fight against any U-boat.

6 January 1941 – I have had two evenings ashore trying to enjoy myself without the means to do so. There is even less to do here than there used to be and there are even more people to do it. Apparently there are 44,000 of the Army alone, quite apart from many more Navy and Army. On Sunday, John and I, after a stroll, had dinner at the Bristol and went to the pantomime. A paymaster sub told us of the raid by the French four months ago. It is an incredible story – that about a hundred French bombers dive-bombed the rock which, only two months before, had given hospitality to men of French destroyers doing convoy work. They haven't done so since, but the relations are still very strange. For instance we stop an occasional convoy in the Straits and sink a submarine bound for West Africa. And yet we let an enormous dry dock, escorted by destroyer, pass through. (At the moment we are being supplied with oranges by the *Charles Plumier* of Le Havre.) We don't know how much longer we shall be here

– presumably not more than a day or two. Two are staying on for two weeks. I must try to walk round to sandy bay before we go.

7 January 1941 – When we were on board this evening, an Army friend of Ellyatt's – a Major – appeared and, after having drunk innumerable whiskies, told us all about the defences of the rock. Apparently a few months ago they were futile. Ironside, who was there are at the time, was just our bluff. He told of how the Frenchman Noques had come over and, having been shown everything and having had lunch, had said 'Well now, my dear Ironside, what about showing me your real defences – after all we are your allies?' One wonders what Ironside's reply was!

A pamphlet, published presumably by the military, came aboard all about Morocco – quite interesting, although mostly obvious. Apparently they – the English – have great faith in Weygand still and think that if anyone can do anything for us then he can. Another thing he said was that the Spanish are starving and friendly 'a great pity that we made such fools of ourselves over Franco'. What in the hell does the fool think we are fighting for?

We may go out tomorrow. It depends whether *Geranium*'s gun is repaired in time. It would be miserable to have to go north again if it isn't.

8 January 1941 – It is quite incredible the amount of drunkenness in this place. I suppose it is partly having been at sea so long but it seems to me largely that the spirits are merely a glorified methylated spirit. Yet they still persist in getting incapably drunk. What pleasure that gives them heaven knows.

9 January 1941 – We had a party tonight, our celebration of Christmas and the New Year. It started at 6.30 when *Cyclamen* and an Army doctor from the *Trooper* came over. Thomas Newall, the Major, appeared, covered in mud having fallen from his bicycle in an undignified puddle. Conversation was a little strained at first but when the others had left we thoroughly enjoyed ourselves – having the Christmas pudding and the champagne, not to mention innumerable other drinks. Afterwards our two piano accordion musicians played for us most excellently, although rather troubled by the presence of the drunk cook. Some of the officers from *Osiris* came over too – the usual type, modest. There we were singing every imaginable

38

well known tune, finishing with the Marseillaise and God Save the King! It was strange to see the electrical effect God Save the King had even on that party at that time of night. At one moment they were laughing, shouting and singing; at the next they were all standing to attention, most solemnly. It was exactly midnight.

**It is perhaps worth recording at that point that we never drank at sea.**

<u>10 January 1941</u> – In the morning went over to *Osiris* to have a look round. Didn't do much looking round but met a Lieutenant Williams RN who remembered me at Prep School at Harrow. I vaguely remember him. It was an interesting morning, if only to meet a submariner. We have lost twenty-seven of our original fifty-four – ten in the Med. Yet they still persist in saying that it is safer than surface craft.

**That afternoon we received our Sailing Orders which follow.**

# SECRET CYPHER MESSAGE
## (OUT)

**ADDRESSED**

C-in-C S.A.
(R)
Admiralty   Clematis (SHM)
Cyclamen. (SHM)

**FROM**

V.A.O.I.A.

**CYPHER**          Small Ships W/T          **DATE**          10/4/44.

A.H. 1716/30/12.   Intend sailing
Clematis Cyclamen for Freetown 1800 11th.
January and retaining Jonquil Geranium
until return of Vees from Freetown.

1242/10/1/41.

Naval Staff                                DC/
Civ. Sec.
G.C.7.

5m. N.S. 10/40 (8794).

# CHAPTER IV

# Southbound

The entries in the diary which follow were written when we were en route from Gibraltar to Freetown to form the Freetown Escort Group. It was a quieter life than we had got used to in the Atlantic, largely because of the different weather, but it is all too clear that often the risks were still considerable. I realize now more than I did then that the Admiralty were very conscious of a possible attack by the German battle cruisers, the *Hipper* or the *Admiral Scheer*. We rather felt that we were regarded as a small target which would alert others to the position of those German capital ships so that they might have time to take appropriate action.

<u>11 January 1941</u> – We left Gibraltar at six this morning. It seemed almost as bad as leaving Rosyth and Liverpool in the old days with just the same rush to catch the mail and, in my case, just the same inability to think of what I want to say. It has a paralysing effect. On our way over we met Force H, rushing in for Saturday evening. They had cut it rather fine though, since they couldn't have been tied up before eight or earlier.

We, as usual, ran into a head wind which, as soon as we had left Cape Spartel, produces quite an unpleasant sea, causing most of us to regret the lazy life we had spent lately. We have had a disaster in the 'straights', running into fishing nets. I saw a few very small lights ahead of *Cyclamen* and decided they must be dhows but they weren't and we had to be quick in getting clear.

Tangier looked most enticing. I wondered what the Rif Hotel is like now and imagined myself strolling out onto the balcony.

<u>13 January 1941</u> – An unpleasant day of which, as yet, there have been no repercussions. It was all the result of my carelessness. The WT Office, in the usual way, suddenly asked for Code 'J' and it was

nowhere to be found. I'm sure it came on board too, quite apart from the fact that it would have been entered in the CB register. After the preliminary panic we had an organized search at four but couldn't find it anywhere and a signal was therefore sent to the Admiralty to which as yet there has been no reply, but it must have turned the Admiralty upside down. I'm afraid it worried the Captain too, which was the last thing I wanted to do. We had all been getting on so well.

**I am afraid I seem to have no record of what the outcome of it all was.**

<u>14 January 1941</u> – Tonight, for the first time, we seemed to be a little nearer to these mythical tropics. I had imagined calm seas with hot sun, but it is still no hotter than a normal June day in England. And the sea is rough. But this evening I went up on deck to have a last look round and the seas had become a little more reminiscent of my dreams. There is a full moon, just appearing over a cloud bank. The wind has dropped, leaving a misty atmosphere which shows up the rays of the moon across the sea. It is now hot enough to walk on deck in shirt sleeves. Yet we still have four days further to go.

The problem of what to do with a French ship arose again today in a signal from the AMC *Marlon*. She reported having difficulty and, to make matters worse, the approach of a French warship. The Admiralty just replied by quoting their original signal, thus leaving the AMC to retreat in as dignified a way as possible if she decided the Frog is too big for her. It is tragic this indecision with the French. Even now we are approaching the Dakar area and the Captain is warned lest something should happen.

# CHAPTER V

# Life in the South Atlantic

<u>18 January 1941</u> – We arrived Freetown yesterday and I've been sweating ever since. Yet it isn't too bad – nothing like as bad as we had been led to believe – and indeed the bathe this afternoon was almost like England again. The Captain and I got a taxi to the beach about ten miles away for thirteen shillings – but I can't write of all this now – there are too many impressions to record. We shall be at sea again in the morning and, after the preliminary panic, I can do so much better then.

<u>20 January 1941</u> – It seems I shall never have a chance to write this up. Today I had thought I could get plenty of peace, but No.1 decided to paint the wardroom, although heaven knows why and we are doing it ourselves. The result was that I was painting steadily from 2 – 6.30. It reminded me of painting the drawing room at home, 'though the scene could hardly have been less similar. – England 1937 and *Clematis* West Coast of Africa 1941

Now I'm desperately tired and its 1 am so I will go to sleep and sweat for six hours.

<u>21 January 1941</u> – Now it is Tuesday evening and all is peace. Last night I couldn't write. All I could do was to read Rimbaud's verse which, as ever, means little to me although for some reason it causes me to keep on mumbling childish English verse to myself – 'I'm quite aware that it's only a chair, yet it does seem quite obscene that it's there.' It <u>must</u> be the heat and general atmosphere of the West Coast of Africa. On the whole, though, I have not seen much. It certainly doesn't seems so attractive as Morocco – of course it is in part but the natives have not the same picturesque qualities. Are they more

43

intelligent? Certainly the half caste in the taxi was – and he had a perfect accent – but the majority seem to be merely cunning. But I have hardly seen them yet, and anyhow how can I hope to know what they are like when there is no chance – or wish – of mixing with them. I suppose I could talk to one of the boys as I did in Tangier but I'm afraid their only interest here is to 'direct you to a very good house, with plenty wine, plenty women'. The drive in the taxi was highly amusing Unlike, I understand, most native drivers, this chap drove with great caution and – without fail – informed every pedestrian of our approach by means of an old bulb horn of which he was obviously very proud. At one stage he, or the car, got wheel wobble, not just ordinary wheel wobble like the old Alvis at home, but a violent shaking which spread even to the back seats – he merely laughed.

It seemed a long way from England; it seemed typical of this hot unhealthy forgotten colony, but I can console myself with the certain knowledge that with the help of the Navy I shall have saved a considerable sum by the time I get back to England – if I do.

Now there seem to be more and more raiders We are not likely to run in to one I hope but if we do – it is best not to think about it.


23 January 1941 – The wardroom is finished at last and looks more like a low down dance hall or the back room of a boarding house which the landlady has tried to 'brighten up'. About all that can be said of it is that at least it is 'different'. It only needs No.1's pair of 12/6 pictures to complete the effect.

We have left the convoy now and are supposed to have met another – the WS5B – but have failed to do so. To make matters worse our 'not met' signal has brought forth a query, having been wrongly cyphered. For once though the Captain was not annoyed – about the only time ironically enough, that it has not been my fault. He's in a good mood now. Poor chap, I don't blame him really, although at times I find it frightfully difficult to forgive his bursts of excessive bad temper. It would be all right if we could be bad tempered with him too but one is, of necessity, at an unfair disadvantage. How childish it will all seem afterwards.

Tobruk has almost fallen apparently and we have now lost the *Achilles*. I wonder if anyone else was there? Turkey doesn't want to come into the war if she can help it – according to Admiralty – but says that she will fight at once in case of aggression.

28 January 1941 – It is intolerably hot. But at least I wrote a few letters – to Mrs O'Donnell and Peter too – and sent off the telegrams. It seems rather futile really, this writing of letters.

Stoker Barker came up to me in the evening, wanting to know how he could get rid of three pounds. Suggested he should put it in the Post Office Savings Bank in *Edinburgh Castle*. Asked him how he liked the Navy. He had done twelve years but then left in 1938 and joined the Merchant Navy doing six weeks in the *Queen Mary* (she apparently rolls very badly). He was separated from his wife but then, when the war started, joined up again – with her and the Navy.

It was a strange and rather misleading life in Freetown in those days. When we were there it was always beautiful weather and ideal for swimming. We often spent some hours on Lumley Beach and also once or twice explored smaller beaches where there was never anybody. The only inhabitants there seemed to be an enormous number of crabs. I well remember arriving once when the whole beach was literally covered in them. When they saw us they scattered. It was indeed a life when one had the problem of that sort of complete peace while you were there but many anxieties when you were not. There were U-boats although not in the same numbers as the North Atlantic. But there were also distinctly dangerous enemy capital ships about. One kept getting signals of sinkings. My diary at that time records the anxiety of expecting to be attacked by one of them at any moment, when of course we would have stood no chance and it would have been Christmas Day all over again. We were fortunate. Our days in harbour were limited usually to two or three only but it was sufficient to give you the chance to relax.

The other peaceful scene which I remember was when, further north, we had instructions to board any French merchant ships that we might see in order to inspect their cargo. It was suspected that in many cases they would have a supply of arms en route for Africa. That was, of course, before the days of Operation Torch, which is recorded later in my diary when serving in *Exe*. When we saw a French ship in *Clematis*, because it was thought that my French was better than that of the other officers, on two or three occasions I was given the job of boarding them. In fact I never found any arms. It was unlikely that I would have found them, but I did have instructions from the Captain to try to make sure that I returned to the ship at least with a case of wine, which I managed to do.

Now we are about to join a convoy – including the *Empress of Australia*, which the Germans claimed yesterday to have sunk.

Perhaps that means they will try to do so, but it doesn't look as if they will have much chance, unless they can produce one of their capital ships such as the *Admiral Scheer*.

29 January 1941 – I am writing this late on Friday. We left early this morning – at 6.0 am. Now I am just drifting as usual. There are thousands of things I should do – mess bills and wine bills which I really must do before we get in, but instead all I do is just dream of all the letters I should write etc. and of all the books I have to read. Today I was looking – no, actually Friday – at the Times Weekly, writing of Halifax, Eden and Margesson.

**Then, rather unusually, I took to a hammock on deck which was peaceful and pleasantly detached from inevitable anxiety about capital ships and U-boats.**

1 February 1941 – I'm sitting in my hammock the sea as calm as ever and the temperature as hot. In fact it is altogether delightful here and could not be improved on even in the best of passenger liners. Yet yesterday evening we had a signal 'There is evidence that a ship was sunk by the *Admiral Scheer* and an Armed Merchant Cruiser [AMC]. That was only in 8N! But still it would all be over fairly soon. *Cyclamen*, *Milford* and ourselves would hardly be able to stay afloat for long.

**The diary entry on 1 February is a good indication of the possibilities we faced. But on the whole I seem to have been pleasantly detached from the cares of the world.**

**One curiosity about the South Atlantic which I have not mentioned but which used to intrigue me was St. Elmo's fire. Given one was near the Equator, on a rather thundery evening you would occasionally get those remarkable lights in the rigging which looked like small blue hurricane lamps. None who has not seen them would believe that they existed but certainly the electrical atmosphere used to produce them – quite extraordinary.**

**We then returned to Freetown again.**

5 February 1941 – In this morning – no raiders seen.

9 February 1941 – It's Sunday today. I have been badly adrift with this diary lately. There has not been much to tell of, but to make

matters worse I am steadily becoming less and less inspired with the will to write every day. Tonight we have been to the pictures in *Edinburgh Castle*. I have had the usual quota of delightful bathing and, what is more important, we have today, Sunday, been inspected by the C-in-C. Not hopeless either, although the ship still looks the dirtiest in the whole fleet.

17 February 1941 – To sea again. I wonder if we shall see the *Admiral Scheer* this time. She is still out there.

19 February 1941 – The wireless is working again – minor excitement this morning when we thought we had found a U-boat. But, after searching for an hour, it ended fruitlessly as usual. There's no news – no news at all. We are just plodding on in the same old way, trying to be cheerful. I suppose it must all end some time.

**There follow again surprisingly resigned reflections on the dangers which clearly surrounded us.**

20 February 1941 – We had news of a raider within a few miles of us this morning and have opened out to ten miles in an extended screen. I'm rather afraid the raider must be looking for us and must know that we only have an AMC for escort. It is significant that there is never any news of them near a heavily escorted convoy. Yet life is still as peaceful as ever.

21 February 1941 – We are now stationed twenty miles ahead of the convoy, still waiting for the raider, the idea being that we should manage to keep it occupied long enough for the convoy to get away before they had been discovered. I suppose *Cyclamen* might come up and help too! I tried to write to M and D this evening but most unsuc- cessfully. But then what can one expect in this atmosphere? I don't expect anything to happen really of course but it would be most unpleasant if it did.

22 February 1941 – A signal from *Glasgow* somewhere north of Madagascar – 'Have sighted Pocket Battleship. Intend shadowing during day and attacking at night.' They now have probably attacked. Poor chaps, many of them won't see day again, if any of them. For they are fighting against heavy odds – they with three triple six inch

47

and the *Admiral Scheer* with eleven inch. It's strange to think of it –
isolated there so far from home where no one knows yet of what they
are trying to do this night. We have turned for Freetown again.

24 February 1941 – We had a little excitement this evening. At seven
we had a good contact and actually dropped three depth charges on
it. And now there really does seem to be some chance of our having
got the U-boat. For the first two attacks it was apparently clearly
moving, but then for the last it was stationary when there were – so
numerous people counted – seven explosions instead of six. Now,
after searching for twenty-four hours we have found large patches of
oil. It was exciting aft and fortunately everything went well, the
Captain expressing his congratulations. Now, with samples of the oil,
we are proceeding at 160 revs excitedly hoping that we may be able
to prove our case. It is not very likely for there should surely have been
some wreckage by now. We were looking so eagerly for bodies too.
It seemed gruesome and I was surprised at myself but for once even I
hoped we would have found some dead bodies.
    It is strange though to think that Felicita's countrymen may have
been killed by the depth charges which I told them to fire.

**Felicita was an Italian girl at Oxford whom my brother and I both knew
and had a very weak spot for. I remember that two brothers of hers were
murdered by the Germans in Italy where, underground, they were doing
what they could to help us.**

27 February 1941 – We had an Admiralty Fleet Order (AFO)today
saying that junior officers could be recommended for service in better
jobs – to put it bluntly – and the Captain, most generously, said he
would recommend John and me. I think he feels rather strongly about
all the decorations recently and would like to do something for us.
No news of the submarine yet but I fear there is not much chance.

28 February 1941 – For some reason I couldn't help thinking of the
possibility of landing on the French or Belgian coast – Brittany or
Ostend – and spending a week snooping around, tonight. I suppose I
would make a complete mess of things – if I ever got there – but I don't
see why it couldn't be possible, with careful planning, to land from
an MTB (that's what put it into my head of course) or a plane into St
Briac. Indeed that would be the best place. At high tide you could slip

right in and get ashore by the Dusuzeau's garden! I wonder if they are living there now and what they would say if I were suddenly to appear. Tragically I doubt if I could trust them.

**The Dusuzeaus were a charming French family with whom I had stayed when I was sixteen. My stay started in Paris before they moved to their house in St. Briac. It was a lovely spot to be right on the coast and also with a golf course inland where I played quite a lot, the French being very hospitable. It is sad that I should have made the comment that I doubted if I could trust them.**

1 March 1941 – Nothing much, still going North to meet the convoy. Tonight it's almost like the NW approaches again, quite cool and a slight head sea. There's a new moon and there's the same old howling of the wind in the rigging which reminds me very vividly of those days from Rosyth. I was talking to John about it on the bridge after dinner and we both agreed that they were indeed ghastly months. I often wonder now how we stood it, standing up there for four hours in the foulest weather, trying to hold on to the convoy and yet not have a collision. And yet now I want to get back there again, probably to even worse conditions and a harder and even more exciting life.

3 March 1941 – Wrote to Peter tonight – the first time since we left.

'Everything I do out here is done in a sort of nightmare frenzy: every evening the three of us, Ellyatt, the Midshipman and I, fool about down here or on deck, doing nothing unless it be to forget where we are and what is happening. In the same way I grasp on this possibility of a change into MTBs, although I know that it can't really be such a peaceful life as this by any means. But now, when it actually happens (with the Raider for instance when I was terrified!) I feel I could willingly do anything once. But I want to write of other things, the peaceful things, and of you, and news of you and home, but somehow I have become para-lysed so that when at last I can write, it is merely of myself. But then there really isn't much to write about except the immediate present. The future and the past both seem so very far off and the future, in any case, is so terribly dependent on the present. And in its turn, of course, so the present is dependent on the future, for few of us could manage to carry on if there were no future to look forward to. There are times, during a quiet night watch for instance, when we have no convoy to worry about, that I think quite normally of peaceful things and of what we will do after the war. Then ambition returns and I feel happy, although I know that when I wake up in the morning I shall have dropped back again to no other thoughts than just the present. Perhaps you feel just the same? But you must feel it so much more too than I, for whom everything still remains a mystery.'

<u>8 March 1941</u> – 'Battle Cruisers *Scharnhorst* and *Gneisenau* in position twenty-one degrees North twenty degrees West.' *Malaya* signalled that she had sighted a Battle Cruiser which was followed by signals from the Admiralty reporting them to be there, ordering Force H and *Repulse* to sea and reporting that *Scharnhorst* had signalled on a submarine frequency. Now Freetown report also picking up signal, considerably nearer – almost on top of us! In fact there is panic in the Navy tonight, particularly as this troop convoy can easily be caught up by the Germans in these days before any reinforcements could possibly get here. And *Phoebe*, *Birmingham* and *Curacao* could hardly hope to deal with two of them I suppose. Or could they? In any case there is bound to be considerable excitement. *Clematis* can't do much so I shall turn in.

<u>9 March 1941</u> – General shuffling of our fleet as a result. *Malaya, Renown, Repulse* will be kept busy. *Furious* is coming down too.

<u>10 March 1941</u> – By simple calculations we may well be within a few miles of them now. There have been signals flying about – one from *Birmingham* saying that as WS6 is probably the objective, hadn't it better split, the fast section going on and the slow creeping along close inshore. C-in-C South Africa doesn't seem to agree, however, and leaves them to their fate, which indeed would be a most unpleasant one, for they could hardly have much chance against the two of them. And there is no question now that there are two, for *Malaya*'s aircraft saw them both, causing *Malaya* to decide on a dignified retreat. So it goes on: perhaps we shall pass them in the night.

Talking of the usual subjects with the Captain, partly prompted by his reading Basil Bartlett's *My First War*. We never say anything now and I nearly always agree with him – 'that we are not fighting for war aims but the very shirts on our backs'. He would be instantly shocked if he knew what I think and write sometimes. Or does he think the same himself occasionally? As he said, war is the last thing he wants, tearing up his life when he had just settled down.

**All was well. In due course we got into Freetown again for a few days, which, I remember, was a considerable relief. The diary indicates that the same dangers still remained.**

<u>19 March 1941</u> – We should have been sailing early tomorrow but something is in the wind and the convoy has been put at six hours' notice. Rumours are flying about – that the *Malaya* has sunk the *Scharnhorst* for instance, but it would seem more likely that she has been sunk herself. Meanwhile there is news that the *Hipper* has left Brest and that the *Rodney* sighted an enemy warship, which she couldn't catch, so it seems more likely that they fear they may all join up together. The whole thing may well bear out what many have said and what the Admiralty must be aware of – that preparatory to spring invasion the Germans are trying to get some of our fleet south. And indeed they will be needed to deal with *Scharnhorst*, *Gneisenau* and *Hipper* and perhaps one other. I wonder what this present scheme is? Then again there is rumour, for the other corvettes have apparently returned to Bathurst instead of here.

Met one of the Free French off a sloop which has come up from Lagos – all typically French and – though they didn't think so – quite lost in an English wardroom. Went ashore and spent a delightful two hours shopping – just like Tangier or Paris. Bought slippers for D and other things which I don't know what to do with, and a crop – which I suppose I might use one day!

<u>21 March 1941</u> – Sailing postponed yet again. Everything was set for six this morning, then postponed till ten and finally indefinitely. We nearly went, but after hanging round *Edinburgh Castle* for half an hour they eventually made up their minds and told us to anchor again. Meanwhile they have been diverting ships into Bathurst. So far as one can gather the cause of the trouble is the *Malaya* business when as well as being torpedoed she was reported as having been attacked by *Scharnhorst* and *Gneisenau*. Little wonder therefore that they don't want to risk a whole convoy. Meanwhile we just await orders which may apparently be for some long time until something else arrives. The most interesting part of it all though is that *Malaya* is going to

51

Trinidad and then on to USA. Are they quite openly going to help us now? My God it looks as if we shall need it at sea. We wait. I'm twenty today. It doesn't seem to make any difference. I'm still the same, there's still a war and it still has to be fought – so the Captain says. We had the usual arguments tonight incidentally.

22 March 1941 – Sailing again postponed. Spent a peaceful day aboard, making our identification signal for the two trawlers which when finished after six hours work were cancelled by *Edinburgh Castle*. Then No.1 and Captain came back with the news that we were going to a dance. I didn't want to go at all but it was worth it after all in that it was a complete change. At first it looked like being a complete fiasco: it looked like a typical 'outpost of the Empire men's club'. There were no girls, only men but at 9.30 the girls arrived and it cheered us up considerably. I even had three dances – two with a very talkative, yet nervous, young lady of at least thirty, and one with a girl who told me that she was a secret agent – both Army nurses and neither out here long. Then when it was just starting they left us in the lurch and we had to cadge a lift back in a lorry affair, generously provided by a member of staff, to find mail waiting for us.

23 March 1941 – Sailed. Seems a dangerously large convoy with no adequate escort, either against U-boats or raiders. Now *Rapello* has been ordered to return to Freetown.

24 March 1941 – 1230 am. Signal from *Malaya* this evening 'At 0200/22 *Marguerite* lost contact. Search was made at dawn but she has not been seen or heard of since.'
   Had been feeling ill on Friday but I think I am recovered now. *Scharnhorst* and *Gneisenau* last sighted on twentieth. Six hundred miles north of Finisterre.

25 March 1941 – From Admiralty to *Mauritius* – 'Raider is *Hipper* or *Admiral Scheer*'. Cheerful for *Mauritius*. It wouldn't be at all surprising if she were the *Admiral Scheer* either, on her way home from the Indian Ocean where she was spotted by *Glasgow*. Anyhow *Bulalo*'s raider report in 7N 24W has caused panic again and *Bulalo* has been told to join us pending arrival of *Repulse* and *Furious*. God knows what would happen if the *Admiral Scheer* got here first: poor old *Aurora* couldn't do much and certainly we couldn't except make

smoke and I don't suppose we could do that for long. What of *Marguerite?*

26 March 1941 – Raider panic still badly on. *Repulse* and *Furious* to join us: at the moment only *Bulalo* and *Aurora*. I think my dream last night must have been largely the result of the depressing 'Road to Bordeaux'.

27 March 1941 – Revolution in Yugoslavia apparently. Presumably that means that the Germans will be in in a day or two.

*Repulse* joined and we feel more secure. It had certainly got to a bad state when the Captain had to say 'Don't challenge anything: wait until I have got to the bridge: challenging can't do any good, if he's enemy we would merely be blown out of the water with the first salvo.'

Captain has been looking at a chart of St. Etienne today, presumably considering having a look in on our way back. I don't suppose we shall. As John said it would be a little awkward if we found the *Hipper* there.

29 March 1941 – Great excitement for half an hour, one of *Furious*'s aircraft having crashed. He misjudged the speed apparently and overran the deck, crashing on the port side. Fortunately we were quite close and, after a few minutes' panic, spotted them. It looked black at first: there was nothing at all to be seen but eventually – I actually – spotted three of them swimming about quite happily. We lowered a boat, picked them up and transferred them to *Furious*. They all seemed to rely on us to do something about it. *Repulse, Furious* and *Maurttius* were all signalling at once. It was an RNVR sub, the pilot.

Great plans are afoot for a raid by the old Clematians on the Port of St. Etienne where the U-boats are suspected of being and where *Delphinium* was told to inspect. The Captain proposes to ask *Furious* to send an aircraft to reconnoitre and if there is one there to ask permission to try to destroy it. I'm afraid it could be a difficult manoeuvre and particularly with what we have at our disposal. It is made even more complicated through the possibility of there being only thirty feet of water which is not enough to set off a depth charge. Getting there, anyhow, could be a risky business. It is a large bay tucked right in behind a jutting out point – a peninsula in fact, half of which is Spanish and half French. There are two possibilities, either

53

to take one of our boats and row the whole way, right into the bay, or to land on the other side of the peninsula, carry a depth charge and rely on finding a native boat the other side. And there is, of course, the alternative of taking *Clematis* right in. But unfortunately it appears that there are a certain number of military there and a shore battery. If they are French they will no doubt be asleep but if the Germans are there they will probably take good care that they aren't. And there are the sub's guns to contend with too. It is possible however and well worth trying. We shall know tomorrow.

30 March 1941 – It was not to be. We had a signal to go to Bathurst instead.

31 March 1941 – We would have been in Bathurst by now, having a peaceful night's sleep, but yet another signal telling us who has the survivors from *Britannia* and also telling us and *Dunoon* and *Foxhound* to intercept her as well as to inform *Dunottar Castle* of her position and if she cannot make it take the survivors ourselves. It is strange indeed that they should make so much fuss about them. There must be someone special there for just merchant seamen could come to no harm in Tenerife, where she is bound. It doesn't look as if we shall find her. According to our calculations we should have met by four. Now it is nine. We are getting very short of fuel too – eighty tons. A description came through of the ship which sank *Britannia*. Apparently an AMC capable of at least eighteen knots. Let us hope she is well out of this area. Had a 'shoot' today with all its inevitable flaps, though not so good as usual. I like guns less and less.

Apparently our fleet action in the Med was a success, sinking three cruisers and two destroyers with the loss of only two AC. If only the Germans could be sunk too. But *Scharnhorst* and *Gneisenau* have got into Brest again.

Captain is growing a beard; I have burnt my leg on the hot pipe in the wardroom.

1 April 1941 – We didn't find her and had orders to return to Freetown so we shan't see Bathurst after all. During the night I was reminded by Pike that it was 1 April and we therefore embarked upon an extraordinarily successful leg pull – I almost feared a bit too good. I got one of the coders to cipher '*Clematis* and *Cyclamen* are to return to the UK by June. It is suggested that they should be used as

additional escorts.' from Admiralty to C-in-C, repeated to us. Then at six it was given to Peter who accepted it, and completely failed to notice the time of origin 0000/1 and actually took it to the Captain who was also taken in and in his turn signalled *Cyclamen*. But *Cyclamen* wasn't taken in, much to the Captain's annoyance. The first I knew of it was when Peter excitedly got hold of me and John to tell us the news. Even then when I pointed out what the time of origin was he didn't see the point. But I thought it probably time to explode it. The Captain was furious at first and the crew even more so. I was by no means popular.

Now we are steering for Freetown with just enough oil. For we had a signal half an hour ago from C-in-C telling us to search for two boat-loads of survivors reported by a Spaniard who has got others. In 11N 23W. Of course it's quite impossible. I wonder what they are survivors from?

2 April 1941 – *Cyclamen* went to look for them. Soon after she had left we had a signal telling us to investigate possible submarine in 11N 20W but even to that we had to reply that we had insufficient fuel; we certainly shan't have more than twenty tons when we get in.

Have been reading *Truth about France* by Louis Levy. It is tragic, telling of all the betrayals by France's leaders and the weaknesses of her leaders in the field. The individual fought like a Trojan as well as anyone in 1914 but so disorganized that no courage could help. But his book can't be quoted, only his quoting of Clemenceau 'War is too serious a thing to be managed by soldiers'.

Delightful example of our attitude during the pre-war days – and the need to preserve a sense of proportion. I hope it still exists.

In at eight tomorrow all being well.

6 April 1941 – I am beginning to suffer from the effect of the typhoid inoculation this morning, my arm being sore and my head hot. Yesterday had a good day with Captain on Hill Station, playing tennis all afternoon and dancing in the evening. We were very lucky too to meet a Colonial Office chap who most generously invited us to dinner, saving our lives since there was nothing to be had to eat otherwise. I could write a lot of the dance but don't feel capable – of the General's wife and of the atmosphere in general and of the art of getting partners.

No I can't write more. The dog has died.

8 April 1941 – Out – *Cyclamen*'s fourteen-day trip was fatal. Having heard of it they have ordered us all to go North of the Azores; as if we have to stay until seventeenth, which will mean a ten-day trip at the very least. Tonight I don't feel like writing of events past and present but of home. I always am the same first day out, particularly when I have had some mail.

Perhaps we may sink a U-boat this time. Two ships have been sunk just at the end of the swept channel. From Weekly Intelligence Reports it is clear that losses are going up badly. How are Greeks and the Turks getting on?

9 April 1941 – I feel miserable tonight. My feelings shouldn't matter; indeed they don't except that as I am I can do nothing else. Yet – and that of course is the reason for it – the Germans are now marching through Yugoslavia; they've taken Belgrade already. They have apparently just flattened the place out and have had no more mercy than before for women and children, just mowing them down with their tanks. I wonder why I think of home; what hope have any of us of getting home, to a real home I mean, for many years yet? My morale is not bad tonight, but how can we beat them by ourselves unless it be after many more years?

10 April 1941 – Have almost made up my mind to volunteer for submarines. The chance seems too good to be missed. I shall certainly be terrified but if I survive it will have been a useful experience. The extra six shillings a day will be good too. But they must be getting short of officers if they will accept us now.

News is getting bad. The Germans are still driving us back and have taken 2,000 prisoners and three generals. If we get driven out of Egypt things will certainly begin to look black. There are Australians there too.

12 April 1941 – Spent nearly all this morning transferring some meat, kindly offered by *Mauritius*. The first try was disastrous in that it got mixed up with the screw and was – all 300 pounds or so – lost. But they persevered and we eventually had three bags for ourselves and two for *Cyclamen* (which we then had to transfer to her). I had the distinction of hooking a bag when morale was low and it looked as if we would have no success at all.

More ships have been torpedoed off Freetown and more attacked by a raider further south. Shall put in a request for submarines when we get in. God knows why really except that I feel it will be good for me and I am just as likely to survive there as anywhere probably. Anyway it should mean England sooner.

Little more news. Our troops are now supposed to be in contact with the Germans though and the RAF is hammering at armoured divisions. I wonder if Ralph is out there? What can Felicita be thinking of it all?

<u>13 April 1941</u> – Bad news tonight. Tobruk has been surrounded now. It looks bad. Where is it all going to end?

<u>15 April 1941</u> – Plugging on. Suspicious vessel, probably raider, reported just alongside us and panic signals from Admiralty of U-boats nearby. Otherwise it is a singularly boring – touch wood – trip. The same routine day after day and the same exercises.

*Bonaventure* has been torpedoed and sunk.

**Strangely my only comment follows. I have no idea why. There does not appear to be any relevance.**

From 'Portrait in a Mirror'  O Mothers of Daughters
Beware when the waters
In winter are covered with ice.

Have burnt my boats over submarines now.

**But it never came off. Instead when we got home I was appointed to *Exe* as A/S (anti-submarine) Officer.**

<u>17 April 1941</u> – Left them at 0600 this morning. It's still uncertain whether we shall go to Bathurst or Freetown – a vote favoured Freetown – but the Captain has reserved his epoch making decision until tomorrow, depending upon fuel. In the meantime 'no canvassing'.

At this stage we are all beginning to become a little bad-tempered but John and I talked this evening in the bathroom of war in general with our usual bad morale. We both agreed – in our usual selfish way – that he and I stood to lose ten times more in this war (like anyone of our age of course) than those like No.1, and the Captain, who have jobs to go back to. Of course John has a certain job but even that is dependent on his father. We must grumble and feel sorry for ourselves

57

occasionally. He insists that he is not at all suited for war and indeed I suppose he is highly strung, but aren't we all?

London has been very badly raided, and Albania evacuated – the poor old Greeks after all their efforts. The Australians are holding on to Tobruk.

Yesterday we sank five transports and five Italian destroyers with the loss of *Mohawk* Am reading *Battle of France*. The first part is tragic in the extreme, to read of the British Army in France in the winter of 1939–1940.

19 April 1941 – News begins to get bad. Last night heard that we have evacuated Albania and are being driven back in Greece, although we are 'inflicting very heavy losses on the Germans'. Tonight it is a little better, we claiming that we are holding them, but it all sounds too like those desperate communiqués from France and Norway for my liking. Bevan said that 'if we can hold out until July we shall then turn the tide; there are three major battles to be won – the Battles of Britain, of the Atlantic and of Greece'. That is a severe change from what we have been saying; there was no question of 'holding out' a month ago.

Today the flotilla has been to manoeuvres with great success. It was in fact quite good fun.

I have not written a single letter. I shan't be able to until I have had some now.

**And so my diary continues. Ships were still being sunk and we were still all too conscious of the dangers of being attacked by one of the German battle cruisers. But we survived. We had a few days from time to time in Lagos and Takoradi. I have a record of some enjoyable hockey against the police in Lagos. I remember particularly playing at right half where I tried to mark the Nigerian outside left amongst others. They were all much too fast for us – particularly the outside left who I found afterwards had won the hundred yards in the annual sports. It was a refreshing break, as was the trip inland up the river from Lagos, which I have recorded later.**

24 April 1941 – Bathed at Lumley and enjoyed myself by myself, reading Sitwell, bathing and strolling along the beach to watch the fishermen hauling in their nets. Otherwise everything is still as trivial as it always is in port, the same petty bickerings and the same futile formalities.

*Oxfordshire* (the hospital ship) is apparently coming back quite definitely and is expected in a fortnight, so should be in by the time we get back. We are going to do a longer trip than ever – eleven days with the convoy, fuelling at Bathurst. We are about due for some more excitement I'm afraid. One of *Anchusa*'s officers said that they were asking for volunteers for submarines when he was there; but still probably they've as many as they want by now.

No letters for some time. Apparently a large majority of mine has been lost too. How futile it all is.

26 April 1941 – Eventually quite a pleasant afternoon, starting badly in that – for our game of cricket – we were unable to get a boat ashore until 2.45 and unable to get off until 7.20. But the cricket was a great success in that we beat *Anchusa* by one run and I made thirty-four in quick time. We only had an hour each way; they went in first and made 125 for I think five, and we made 126 not out. We didn't have our hour really though and although finally it was our score which appeared suspicious, I suspect strongly that their scorer must have a stuck a few on to their score for it certainly appeared that they were scoring considerably faster. The Captain of *Anchusa* is a strange character indeed – an RNVR Lieutenant from colliers running between Newcastle and Shoreham who got the DSO in Norway in a trawler. He tells thoroughly amusing stories with fine verisimilitude – of the trawler from Belfast for instance which was continually running aground and to which NOIC sent a signal when she was due to go to Oban – 'Proceed to Oban by sea'.

We sail at 0500, but fortunately I haven't to turn out. This time we go further west still – thirty-two degrees and two days longer.

I have burnt my submarine boats now. Perhaps I shall hear something next time in, probably not.

27 April 1941 – Have just had signal, supposedly of great secrecy but only in code, saying that the American fleet is at sea in the Atlantic, north and south. They will not, it is said, take part in any naval action between Germans and ourselves but should they see enemy raider will follow and report its position every four hours. Non-Recognition procedure is to be brought into force and they will proceed with or without lights at their discretion. Is it just a huge bluff or is it the first step to their coming in? If only one of their ships would get itself torpedoed!

<u>28 April 1941</u> – Athens occupied by the Germans announced today. Churchill spoke, usual fighting speech apparently but preparing us for evacuation of Greece. Explained that we had completely miscalculated the number of Germans in Libya. We only had 30,000 there. Germans are suggesting by propaganda that we have again put all the fighting on to someone else – this time the Australians. Also claiming that there is dissatisfaction in bad areas. Churchill himself had been round and is convinced that spirit is better than ever. Read *Battle of Britain* this morning, demonstrating more clearly than ever before how badly Ribbentrop miscalculated – not to mention Goering.

From C-in-C, South Africa: 'Enemy S/M has made first sighting report, probably S.L.73'!

<u>29 April 1941</u> – Turkey has made a trade agreement with Germany – for machinery. At least there is the consolation that there is no other country one need worry about, but it is a little disconcerting. Should we just withdraw all our troops from abroad and concentrate on protecting England? It would mean that, unless America came in, we could have no chance of winning for an interminable time but what good will they do where they are? Plymouth has been evacuated. Liverpool is our only working port left.

<u>30 April 1941</u> – I wonder how long it will be before we do have another shot at Dakar – that is if we can spare the ships now, which is doubtful. Leakey's friend, Huntley, from *Dunedin* said that *Dunedin* has been out doing landing exercises and night shoots and that they are due to go out with her for searchlight practices. That may be – though it is a small point – why C-in-C said that we were to have one and certainly links up with what the Captain said.

<u>2 May 1941</u> – The last two days have been very energetically spent painting this cabin and it is 12.45 am. We have got 42,000 out of Greece, 8,000 having been taken prisoner (how wretched to be taken prisoner there with the prospect of being killed on the way back to Germany) and we are having trouble in Iraq already.

Painting this cabin was a dreadful effort but it certainly looks very nice indeed now and at least five times lighter. This off-white paint is a great success.

Went badly off the boil this evening unknown to anyone else and completely losing my bearing when the convoy altered course at ten. I don't quite know how it happened but I soon realized that I had no idea exactly where they were. Thank God I found everything again though – just before the moon went down and the Captain came up. Must have been very tired – certainly am now.

3 May 1941 – There is a hush before the storm and a diary seems pointless. Any diary after all is only a chronicle of past events – or should be. No point in writing now when the news has still to come. The war for us here is still the same. We still have found no U-boat, we still have our monstrous and irritating meals, we still 'go to exercises' at 5.15 and generally fool about until 6.00, then having a bath or taking sights purely for propaganda purposes. We still wait for the day when we shall meet the *Bismark* and the *Admiral Scheer* at once, alone or with an AMC. But elsewhere there is this hush. We are out of Greece successfully and everyone wonders what will happen next. There are signs of trouble in Iraq, the report being that they have bombarded our aerodromes and, in BBC language 'Raids on England are being intensified'. So it goes on but how much longer?

Meanwhile I have the afternoon off and shall read peacefully. I should like a game of tennis on a certain bumpy lawn surrounded with fruit trees and roses.

**I am referring there to the grass tennis court at home on which we often used to play.**

2100 – Two more destroyers lost in Greek evacuation, the AMC *Voltaire* and what else? Yet at dinner tonight we were talking – perhaps a little forced at times – of golf, rugger (the Harlequins and their Welsh tours) and I was thinking of school, the Spartans and the games against the London Irish. One is thought to have bad morale if one thinks of this war as I do sometimes; in fact I feel almost ashamed of myself if I do.

Fighting in Iraq continues, *Diamond* and a VW* lost with fifty survivors and South African troops being taken from Abyssinia to reinforce Libya.

---

* Destroyers whose names began with V or W, as in *Vansittant* and *Wishart* for instance.

<u>5 May 1941</u> – No news so far as we are concerned except that we leave at 0600 tomorrow. It has been a long trip. News tonight that the *Scheer* and the *Gneisenau* really have been hit by Coastal Command. All of them got back too: it makes me feel very strongly for that friend of John's who got shot down. It is so tragic that they don't get more decorations too. It seems that the Navy have perhaps had more than their fair share, particularly during the Norway business. The Captain certainly deserved his DSO, but I cannot help feeling that the RAF should perhaps have had more recognition for what they did. The Coxs'n gave me a most extraordinary cutting from some paper purporting to be a prophecy made by a Saint 'Someone' in 713. It is right in every respect about Germany, saying that the peak of her success would be reached eighteen months from the outbreak etc. I will copy out some extracts in the morning. I have had to return it to the Coxs'n now. But it was quite extraordinary.

Now we are off on our own. *Surat* torpedoed 8N 15W.

<u>6 May 1941</u> – Have been writing to Diana and having been reading *The Spirit of Paris* which she gave me, feel very Paris-sick. 'But I would so love to be walking with you down the Avenue Victor Hugo which is the part of Paris I know best, in the early morning setting out just to wander haphazardly round the shops, to have a glorious lunch of apple pie and then perhaps to be real trippers and have a taxi to Fontainebleau or Versailles, or perhaps the great Robinson.'

Yes, I was feeling very sentimental but I managed to write more intelligently than usual in the end. I wrote to M and D too and had my ritual bath.

<u>7 May 1941</u> – 'With every roll
　　　　　we get further from
　　　　　that goal —
　　　　　of half-forgotten dreams which
　　　　　always seem
　　　　　quite senseless.'

This shows the sort of mood I'm in tonight. Quite suddenly during dinner I felt like it, remembering in a few seconds all my childish ambitions, all those things the war has spoilt for me. I felt I must write a thoroughly miserable letter to someone and started one to Peter but I have only written four lines. It will pass of course: when

I get up at midnight I shall have forgotten about it all, but now—

Today has been an annoying day too. Last night we had a signal telling the Captain to detach two corvettes to the assistance of the *Ashbury* which had sent out an SOS and was only doing three knots. The Captain had to decide that we must all go even though we have got nothing like enough fuel which necessitated doing only eleven knots, thus not getting there until Friday morning. *Cyclamen* was to have gone but she insisted that a faulty shaft in her engines could cause serious damage at fifteen knots, so *Marguerite* went instead. Countless ships have been sunk round here lately. *Dorsetshire* has picked up survivors and *Dragon* was sent for more but has reported herself short of fuel. What about us? We can only do ten knots and won't get in until Sunday.

8 May 1941 – Found this morning that we only had seventy-five tons left, having used twenty-three and eighteen tons in the last three days. There are 900 miles to go so, at the rate of eight tons to one hundred miles we would have one ton to spare. Therefore Bathurst eventually decided on. (*Cyclamen* on being asked whether she was coming replied 'Yes please') and course set to pass delightfully close to Brava and Fogo. It was a most delightful surprise for me; I knew they were there but I hadn't been on deck all the morning and when I did go up at two they were just abeam, only three miles off. Brava has 9,000 inhabitants and Fogo 2,000 (according to the pilot) but heaven knows where they all live for from the ship at least we could only see, on Brava, a few houses right along the top – about 4,000 feet up. They look very barren and wild, just like the Hebrides, and indeed reminded me very vividly of those days. It was so delightful to see high rocky hills again too.

9 May 1941 – *Cornwall* has sunk a German raider in the Indian Ocean, fifty-seven Germans and twenty-three British saved. Raids over England are getting progressively worse and it looks rather as if it might be leading up to some new plan. Twenty-six planes were brought down in one night and we sent four to five hundred to bomb Hamburg. I hope we did.

10 May 1941 – We got into Bathurst at ten this morning, having made our ETA as 1300 so as to give ourselves a bit more time. I had had the middle watch and therefore didn't go on deck until we were

63

nearly in. It was a most exciting and refreshing scene as we steamed in, being far more like, as Ellyatt and I both agreed, some East Coast river than the Gold Coast. It might have been Waldringfield for instance. The town itself looked at from the river is clean and pleasantly laid out, whilst in a little bay there were over a dozen fishing boats anchored, lying just off the mud banks from which jetties run out, old wooden ones, broken down. It wasn't so hot either and might well have been a hot summer's day and *Clematis* a small sailing boat.

The day was a great success. We had finished oiling by lunchtime and leave was given to the sailors from 1300 – 1700. John and I managed to slip No.1, going ashore a little later in our own boat. We wandered round the town first, quite different from Freetown, a thousand times cleaner (in its inhabitants as well) and almost European in parts, with grass paths by the side of the road – surprisingly green – clean houses with very pretty gardens full of flowers which could only be found in the richest greenhouse in England. Nor did the natives worry us. We went into a small shop attracted by some wooden spoons and forks, which we bought for twopence each, but even there there was no question of bargaining. Then, hot and tired, we made for the beach where we met No.1 and bathed. Finally the Captain unexpectedly turned up to tell us that we were invited to the Governor's for tennis and that he had brought rackets and shoes. The house and grounds bore out all that I had thought about the white man's grave – a perfectly comfortable house, beautifully furnished and magnificent gardens better than you could hope for in England, with a grass and hard tennis court. The Governor himself fitted the part well – Scottish – but his wife, though suitable in other ways, had a disconcerting squint so that even if you were as much as ten yards away from the person addressed you imagined her to be addressing you. And vice versa, when trying to talk to me, I thought she was talking to my next-door neighbour. But the tennis was thoroughly good fun. Finally the Army invited John and me to dinner with them, talking the while enthusiastically of other dinners and celebrations they had with the Navy, particularly *Mauritius*, regaling themselves with vast quantifies of drink. But we stood up to it all right and arrived back safely none the worse for wear, although – after being very careful all the evening – I nearly killed myself by drinking a glass of neat gin by mistake. We kept the Captain waiting ten minutes in the boat, but he couldn't very well be bad tempered.

It was typical of the Captain to think to bring tennis rackets and shoes so that we might play tennis together. What I have occasionally described as his bad temper was simply the natural expression of his anxiety and the understandable feelings of a much older man whose responsibility was so much greater than ours.

16 May 1941 – Yet again I had to leave this, quite unable to get any time to myself until this evening, when I wrote letters. The last few days have been very hectic, not at all peaceful but also enjoyable. The only amusing or interesting incident I can remember was the affair when the Frenchmen's boat sank, though not until they had just managed to get here. The one I spoke to mostly, a certain Capitaine Tourot, was a colonial official who has been out here since the war started but whose family is still in Bordeaux. He was delightfully French, complaining typically (admittedly at my instigation) that we had not brought in conscription early enough and we had suffered from out of date English traditions. He thought there was a subtle difference between that and being 'paresseux'. Anyhow he, a Commander and his wife are coming to dinner tomorrow so no doubt we shall hear plenty then. I fear it will be a sever strain but it may be amusing.

Otherwise little has happened. Last night Richards and the Captain's Secretary came to dinner and Greenfield and some RNR paymaster came in afterwards, all of them staying until the ungodly hour of twelve, and I had to spend nearly the whole evening trying to entertain Richards who had had far too much to drink, putting down one whisky after another.

In the afternoon we all went up to play tennis at Hill Station. Now the Captain has asked me to be No.1. I wanted to refuse; it will mean a lot more work, and John certainly wanted me to – but I didn't, so unless C-in-C has other plans, I am doomed. I only pray that the other sub who comes may be an expert in gunnery. Anyhow my application for submarines has now gone in officially and I have passed the medical so something may come of that soon – two months perhaps.

17 May 1941 – I had not been looking forward to last night – the strain of having the Frenchmen in our wardroom – but, apart from one minor disaster, the evening was quite a success. Unfortunately the Commandant's wife found the motion of the ship and the

considerable heat of the wardroom too much for her and had to ask to be put back ashore again. But she did it so delightfully gracefully with typical French ease. I took her back in the boat and enjoyed that half hour more than any for a very long time, walking up to her house with her, talking quite easily – far more easily than I had expected. She was so charming and gave me a Free French brooch as a memento. The dinner too was not bad. I had bought some Cape wine in the afternoon for only one shilling a bottle which was better than I had expected and at best helped to give some sort of atmosphere. Our only trouble was shortage of space but I got over that by taking the extension from the Captain's desk and pushing it on to the table, resting it on the radiator. I don't remember much of what they said and anyhow I can't write of it now in the middle of a panic to get ready for an inspection and I had to be up at six this morning too.

1400 – The C-in-C came and went, as nervously and as quickly as he could. His inspection of the Port Division perhaps rather put him off. Later he addressed the men, obviously having no idea of what he was going to say, eventually comparing the Sahara Desert to the North Western Approaches. Perhaps it was all best summed up by Scott who, in his usual way, said that he gathered from those who had heard him that he had had a little to drink before he came.

Now we have had orders to proceed on patrol. No sooner were we outside the boom than a ship was torpedoed right on the line *Bridgwater* and ourselves were supposed to be patrolling. We have been looking for the survivors and U-boat since but now *Bridgwater* has just picked them up (sixty-four) How long we shall stay out here we don't know – presumably four to five days, all the time darting from one phoney position to another burning thirty tons of fuel a day.

19 May 1941 – I feel, as I do periodically, worried tonight by my completely inadequate knowledge to do the job I'm doing. I was disturbed, I suppose, by the story of *Columbine*'s and *Godetia*'s collisions, both of them largely due to an inexperienced OOW (in *Columbine*'s case she had a collision with *Aberdeen* when doing a ninety degree turn the wrong way through 270). Tonight we are just wandering up and down this patrol line with orders to escort any ships

we may come across to within fifty miles of Freetown. I only hope we don't run into *Bridgwater* or one of the others and if we do that Lecky has got the identification signals right; we don't want a broadside from one of them.

News tonight that an Egyptian ship used as an Anglo-American hospital ship, expensively fitted out by the Americans is overdue at Cape Town since 27 April. Presumably it was a raider.

I wonder what chance there is of our refitting in America – none at all of course, but it is a good thought, particularly when the Admiralty start making signals that civilian clothes should be worn by officers when ashore. The Captain quite seriously talks of getting one of his suits sent out – the not-so-well-cut one!

The calendar changed yesterday – the Lake District near Coniston.

Then we had orders to rendezvous *Columbine* and meet NJ8FS presumably in 18N. But *Columbine* failed to turn up at the rendezvous. Later she signalled that her engines had broken down but that she was following at fifteen knots; then again that she had picked up sixteen survivors from a Dutch trawler but that her engines had finally broken down again and she was returning to Freetown. Sinkings are certainly getting considerably worse and it looks very much as if they will have to do something drastic such as start the convoys from Lagos or even the Cape – calling in on Freetown to fuel – if they are going to improve matters. A few ships on patrol will never do any good.

21 May 1941 – Now Crete has been invaded but the position is 'well in hand' – although there are still admitted to be 1500 Germans at large! They arrived by troop carriers, dressed in Canadian battledress. Now (by which time 3,000 more are admitted to have landed) the Germans say that if we are so brutal as to treat them as spies they will shoot ten to every one we do. Of course we shan't shoot them and the next news will be that Crete has been successfully evacuated. The shipping losses the following week will be very high, but Crete will be used as a convenient excuse – 'but that includes 200,000 tons lost in the Crete evacuation,' they will say.

Tomorrow we should meet them. *Asphodel* and the two new A's have been also told to too as a result of a great inspiration by someone in operations. Even then they forgot to tell them in the first signal even what the convoy's position was.

Today we mustered the Confidential Books to my agony, but I must have done well for all the Captain said was, 'I must say, laddie, the CBs were as good as I thought they were'.

There are a lot of letters I must write.

23 May 1941 – 0030 News of Crete is bad. *British Grenadier* has been torpedoed in 6N. Germans are said to have landed waves of parachutists etc. and a thirty-ship convoy is somewhere about, so far having only been attacked by our light forces, losing two ships and a destroyer. In fact, what with the fast-growing crisis here and imminent evacuation there, I had best go to sleep.

We met them all right this morning with inevitable panic of action stations bell. There are only two and two AMCs and they are doing fourteen knots so we should be in on Sunday – in time to be out again on Monday.

23 May 1941 – Position in Crete is getting worse and it looks as though they are preparing us for Naval losses, talking of the difficulties of dive-bombing. That is no longer an Englishman's traditional game.

Signal from *Anchusa* to C-in-C 'Ran aground Bijol Shoal 0505; refloated 0545, carried away dome and oscillator.' Obviously his navigation is as primitive as *Amaranthus* after all who didn't even go through the boom to get into Freetown but scraped across the mud round the corner and lost her dome too.

30 May 1941 – It is now Friday. During the last few days I have almost forgotten about this diary. Not that much has happened – very little has but I have been in that difficult state when I have written no letters even. Perhaps it was due to *Oxfordshire* coming back. If it was it was subconscious – a subconscious reminder of civilization again and of all that we are missing here. Before she came back, I was happy to go up to Hill Station with John and play tennis, as we did on Monday. But now (it will only be temporary) I am reminded of the simple things one used to do to amuse ourselves, things which then were merely boring but now could be exciting. Gwen, with her accounts of simple pleasures in South Africa, reminded me. I met her yesterday, after long exchanges of signals, and we went out together, although sadly only for a short while as she had to catch the early boat. We were going alone but Elizabeth turned up with a doctor from *Dragon* so we gave them a lift in our taxi.

68

It was delightful. Gwen brought me more books – particularly Housman – and told me all about the Cape. She told me at very great length and would, I am sure, still have been telling me now. We may not meet again. Their reliefs sailed a week ago and we shan't be back for a fortnight at least. I hope they won't have gone. I should like to go out with her once more and I should like to give her messages and letters to take home for me, as well as parcels. It will be like saying goodbye to civilization again too.

Naval news has been certainly startling. First the *Hood* was sunk by the *Bismark* and then two days later the *Bismark* was, nearly the whole fleet being out after her. There have been bad losses in Crete where the Army is again distinguishing itself. We have already lost three cruisers and about five destroyers. It seems inevitable that we shall withdraw again. But Roosevelt has delivered a state of National Emergency.

Local news to *Clematis* is that reliefs – or additional complement – have sailed for four corvettes including us, ours being S.L. Cripps RNVR. It looks therefore very much as if No.1 will get home and I shall get his job, which will be disastrous. If only it were my relief. Otherwise there was nothing until this morning when it was discovered that Scott and another had left the ship with the skiff, having broken into the spirit room and pinched a bottle of rum. There was considerable panic. We oiled and then began a search, finally retrieving them when we had almost given up hope tied up to the oiling jetty. Seven days each I suppose.

We had old Cochrane to lunch on Wednesday – fine old chap – and *Asphodel* told his story of the Court Martial of which Cochrane quite rightly I suppose refused to consider a joke, telling *Asphodel* off for being amused at it (*Calendula* signalled to *Asphodel*, stupidly through *Dorsetshire*, 'My asdic is buggered up'). *Dorsetshire* reported him to C-in-C and he is to be court martialled apparently.

31 May 1941 – Not unexpected news that Dakar has been occupied by the Germans. They landed sixteen mechanized units from a French ship. How many a unit is I don't know, but presumably they can't be more than three thousand in all. Yet that would be enough to take Bathurst and certainly enough to hold Dakar whilst air bases are established – though I don't quite know where the planes could be flown from. Presumably U-boats will use it openly too.

We stay with this lot until the seventh, and then return to Freetown via Bathurst for fuel. Time seems to pass more quickly now. And they are certainly better off now that they have the wireless set, bought from *Anchusa* for twelve pounds. I feel less tired now too. Last night I kept on finding myself nearly asleep and felt ready by midnight. *City of Durham* is twenty miles ahead of us though heaven knows what she is expected to do with her eight four-inch.

1 June 1941 – An exciting morning meeting and boarding French convoy of three ships escorted by sloop. An altogether extraordinary day. I might now well have been wandering up and down the bridge of that Frenchman or scrabbling about in the engine room, the six of us trying to keep the ship going. It would have been a tiring experience but I was resigned to it. It could indeed have been magnificent to have sailed her into Freetown with the other two and anchored, flying Scott's white ensign.

The sleep from four to eight is always the best and that morning when we were far enough north for it no longer to be uncomfortably hot, I was particularly comfortably asleep when the action bell went at a quarter to six. Needless to say I was late getting on deck, struggling to change out of my pyjamas. Even at that hour though, I recognized the French destroyer and realized the position. By extraordinary chance we had run straight into a French convoy of three 4,000-ton ships escorted by this sloop. Everyone became excited. *Amaranthus* signalled, 'Shall I open fire on them?' and steamed to cut them off one way whilst we did the other. But they didn't stop and, whilst we exchanged vague signals with the unhelpful *Moreton Bay*, I expected some excitement. Eventually it was definitely decided that, in spite of the sloop, we should capture all three but *Moreton Bay* refused to provide boarding parties and insisted that only two corvettes should stay.

Meanwhile *Amaranthus* was still anxious to open fire and *Columbine* and *Asphodel* were coming up astern. But *Asphodel* was ordered to rejoin. We and *Amaranthus* went up alongside the Frenchmen and ordered them to stop. One didn't do so, so we fired across his bows. Still he didn't (in spite of my entreaties in French through the microphone which I found a severe strain), so we fired again, this time with the Lewis. Finally, after telling the sloop that there would be trouble, he stopped and I got the boarding party ready for what seemed a harebrained and not to say dangerous scheme. There were eight of us – myself, Mitchell, Milne, East, Berry, Christian, Scott and another armed with revolvers (four), rifles (two), a Lewis gun and as much ammunition as we would ever be able to use. Scott had an ensign, semaphore flags and a Very pistol. We were excited at the possibility of getting back to Freetown a long time before *Clematis* who proposed rejoining the convoy.

They had at last put a ladder over but it was two or three feet too short so that (fortunately it was almost calm) we had a struggle getting on it. I left them to get all the arms etc. out of the boat and went straight to the bridge, wondering what on earth I was going to say or do. At that time everyone, except the passenger and his wife, looked hostile. The Captain and officers were on the bridge. I was as polite as possible but he refused to shake hands – not that I expected him to – and when I asked him what he proposed to do said that the engines were '*saboto*' in any case and was in every way obstinate and unhelpful. But there was no sign of anyone attempting to cause any difficulty on deck, so I sent one of those who came aboard with me to round everyone up in the engine room and aft, collecting them all together on the boat deck. The Captain had by that time become surprisingly polite and we had a great party comparing their numbers with the numbers on the list, which I had. I then had a look at his cargo lists – for something to do – and noted the supplies of petrol, all of which he swore was for Porta Baret.

There was then little else left to do other than get down to the more important business of getting them all out of the way (those of them, that is, who absolutely refused to help) and getting the ship going again. For *Clematis* had gone, we having replied that we were all right. Obviously the sooner we got out of the position the safer for us. But Berry reported two steam pipes broken.

I wanted to find out who was definitely against us and who might be with us so, to gain time, I told the Captain that we could organize meals for everyone, provided they all kept together. They still behaved very well and the Captain was still stubbornly polite when I called him over and asked him what his attitude was going to be. But he replied firmly, complaining that we had killed so many Frenchmen before their ships had even had time to get up steam. Nothing I said made any difference. He showed me his medal and spoke of fighting with the English. The Chief Mechanic was the same, flatly refusing to do anything at all and having no excuse for the stoppage, finally merely saying that he was doing his duty and I mine. He would not explain why it was his duty and, like the Captain, denied that it was an order from the Vichy government.

They, except for the wireless operator, were the only ones I had any time to talk to. The wireless operator just showed me his cabin – which he is presumably still locked out of as I still have the key – and asked me if I was going to smash the set. He seemed to expect me to do so. Meanwhile they were having a good meal and celebrating with wine (I could hardly imagine a German boarding party encouraging them to sit down peacefully to a meal but it seemed by far the best thing to do when everything was still uncertain and in any case we had, it seemed then, plenty of time to play with). We had signalled the position to *Clematis* and the Captain replied that he proposed sending a report to C-in-C asking that an escort be sent out to meet us.

It would have been a most extraordinary party, especially if the sloop had stayed with us. It could have been a nightmare too, of course, struggling round the ship in the dark with no torch – or if we had got going by then, keeping station on the others. And there could have been the fun of scrambling into Freetown, through the boom, anchoring in the approved anchorage.

As it was, at nine o'clock (I suppose we had been aboard about an hour and a half) saw *Clematis* coming back again, although Scott swore that it was another French destroyer. She signalled that she was sending a boat and that convoy was to proceed so we collected all our goods and chattels together again – the Lewis gun had been almost repaired by then – and I went to say goodbye to the Frenchmen, who by that time were having a glorious meal. All the Captain said was thank you and told the crew that they could now eat in peace. I wished him good luck and wondered how long it would be before he got back to Brittany – which he and I both knew.

We scrambled down the ladder as dangerously as we had come up it and arrived back on *Clematis* to find the flap and bad temper in full swing. The Frenchmen were still stopped when we last saw them. I hoped the Chief Mechanic of the *Turs* was having a hot time repairing the steampipes.

2 June 1941 – After all that we had orders to meet the St. Vincent ships. It meant leaving a convoy of fifty-five with only two escorts but apparently there are so many U-boats round the Cape Verde Islands that they considered it worthwhile. Anyhow they have ordered all British merchant ships to keep clear and three ships have been torpedoed in the last two days going in and out. We are supposed to arrive in daylight and search until 2200 when the ships come out. We have

to keep outside territorial waters but if we get a contact we can attack.

Crete has been evacuated now. The Germans are said to have been landing 5000 a day from troop carriers.

3 June 1941 – A wild goose chase. After all of the panics, during which fishing boats were mistaken for something worse, we arrived off the channel at five and patrolled up and down. As soon as it began to get dusk, we went in – inevitably inside territorial waters – and optimistically waited for them to come out. We waited in vain until half past nine when we went outside to the rendezvous and wandered about for the rest of the night, the Captain obviously worried lest we should get torpedoed. At two a signal came through in Interdepartmental cipher – for which I had to be woken – saying that the ships had not sailed but that U-boat had been reported in such a position, exactly where we had been and indeed probably ourselves. We were instructed to hunt it and await further orders though they warned us that we might be wanted to escort the *Kingston Hill* southwards. So we are still here, on what might easily be a ten-shilling tour of the islands in some luxury liner's motorboat. I hope we don't stay long. There is something intensely sinister about their barrenness and extraordinarily high peaks (some 8,000 feet). I wonder if they will be as deserted in a year's time. Only today there is news that the Germans are going to take over the French African ports which presumably include Casablanca and Dakar. But it seems clear that the Americans are on their toes – even now MVs in Freetown report having seen considerable US units.

4 June 1941 – We are to escort *Kingston Hill* to 12N and then return to Freetown, presumably just in time to take the next Sierra Leone. She comes out at 0200 and we have to meet her in the same rendezvous at 0330 by which time the moon will have gone down. I have the awkward watch again.

Spoke to an Argentine ship this evening who was very friendly. We have never met anyone like it before and were most cheered by the waving of hands and handkerchiefs. There aren't many and there are then fewer who are willing to appear friendly. I wonder if we shall see the mysterious fifth columnists again tonight. The *Yeoman* is quite convinced that there were evil men at work.

5 June 1941 – We still await *Kingston Hill*. For two nights now we have waited for her at the rendezvous without success, but we still have

no signal from C-in-C. In the meantime we continue this tour of the islands, which now we have done from almost every possible direction. It becomes tedious and I find myself getting depressed by it – by the very peacefulness of what almost seems a different world from ours.

6 June 1941 – This was definitely to be our last day. Still we had no signals and were even unable to transmit any, but we had just enough oil to hang on. Nothing turned up though, so we are now on our way back empty-handed. It was a strange and perhaps dangerous business patrolling that same rendezvous every night for four nights, but apart from the two survivors, from one of the torpedoed ships presumably, we found nothing.

America has gone one step further and requisitioned all merchant ships in American ports, including the *Normandie*. It is not yet clear what she proposes to do with them, but they will surely come to us in the end. What delightful confusion there will be when the war is over and they all have to be accounted for.

It seems certain that this will be No.1's last trip. He had, he says, another row with the Captain yesterday and told him straight out that he wanted to go. We all become so childish now, each knowing exactly what the other is going to say whatever his reaction to anything will be.

Propose to get rid of the mess bills and CBs for good now, particularly as this morning I find I am probably six pounds out of pocket. It is entirely my own inefficiency but it is for that none the less annoying.

8 June 1941 – More torpedoings – *Adda* and *Elmdene* last night. *Cyclamen* is out towing in *Adda*'s lifeboats – she went just at the end of the major channel. Takoradi and Lagos are closed too through mines, so it looks as if they will have to start doing something pretty quickly out here. We shall probably go straight out again to meet WSX in 16N.

Arrived Bathurst at 2000. Met *Velox* going out. They asked where *Aster* was. In best corvette traditions she has lost herself. Perfect this evening – completely peaceful, with a full moon and no wind. And we are anchored right close in to the shore.

9 June 1941 – We should have sailed this afternoon with the *New Northland* – registered Quebec – who acts as our Army transport, but

74

the Army has charge and sailing has therefore been postponed until tomorrow pm. Having loaded up with odds and ends it has now been decided that they must be unloaded again. And she has aboard some unfortunate chaps from Gib who, homeward bound in *London* were down here, looking for the *Bismark*'s supply ships, transferred and are now bound for Freetown! They must find it disturbing and now the Army and everyone here are in a great panic lest the French and Germans will take reprisals for Syria, which they could do easily. The Army are accordingly on two hours' notice – presumably to evacuate. Lord Louis Mountbatten was here today though, and it was presumed that he had been sent for some very secret mission (at least to strengthen morale) but the Captain had lunch with him and the Governor and it transpired that he was only on passage from the Battle of Crete to London. Presumably he was Captain of *Kelly* when she went – the third he has lost. The Captain said he looked the part magnificently but was obviously on edge. There were hush-hush Americans there too, but they have all gone off in the Civil Flying Boat so Bathurst is not going to gain. We went ashore and enjoyed ourselves pottering round the town and bathing. I bought a fez and an earthenware jar, Moroccan although I didn't know it at the time, which appealed to me although pretty broken. It is good and should look well in England.

In fact there is great panic here, not reduced by a French plane flying over on the afternoon and again now. They must be up to something I'm afraid.

10 June 1941 – We sailed from Bathurst at 1500 with *New Northland* and *Belgravian* who asked if he could join up with us. Her Captain was in *Assyrian* when she was torpedoed in the famous SL convoy and went on firing her four-inch although broken in half and sinking. She was still firing when she went down, having fought the U-boat for forty minutes. God knows how this Captain survived, very few did and certainly the old Commodore was badly injured. Tonight I feel homesick and rather miserable – stupid of me but there it is.

12 June 1941 – Arrived Freetown today, concentrating chiefly on Gwen and *Oxfordshire*. Perhaps that was why the Captain decided his officers were lacking in intelligence when he made a complete mess of going alongside the oiler. Then I found that Gwen had already embarked in *Scythia*, thereafter spending what might have been a

miserable afternoon on board whilst it poured with rain. Nor did the great Cripps arrive, Edward Blyden having been diverted to Takoradi.

13 June 1941 – Again concentrating on Gwen from whom I had now heard, with a vague invitation to go over by getting in touch with *King* who could provide the boat, they being sure they wouldn't sail on Friday, 13th. It was a great success, so much so that it is difficult to write of. Yet there was always that tragic atmosphere of the last goodbye on the station platform type, particularly when Gwen and I were sitting on the couch in the writing room after tea. I think we both felt the same. I think we both were conscious of the same trivial details – and we both felt the atmosphere was totally unreal. It was unreal; it was cruelly so. There was she going back to England, obviously frightened lest they could be torpedoed, and there was I longing for all those things of which she was dreaming too (flowers and fields and the smell of cars) but faced with not seeing those things for many months. And all the time too I think we both kept asking ourselves what conditions we would meet in next. Could it be Hasler and Fort Blockhouse? But the time came to leave and I felt I was saying goodbye to England so I shook hands with her on the gangway.

Then there was an unholy flap – a signal to *Vindictive* 'Palmer to return immediately' and we came back to find the ship under sailing orders, half the crew at the pictures – motor boats, stores – chaos in the dark – and then heard at 2400 that we wouldn't be needed until 0550/17.

14 June 1941 – Now we are ready to take three troopers south.
There is no glory in war; it is all hard work. Perhaps reading Stephen Gwynne's Biography of Scott should have made me feel differently, but life has suddenly begun to seem pointless again fighting to preserve an old world order and not, as Scott fought, to discover something new. We are discovering nothing new, merely fulfilling every day an age-old fact – that man cannot live together without fighting. Scott did, just because he had something else to fight instead.

16 June 1941 – There was something tiring about this convoy, something depressing – perhaps tiring because it was going so fast and zigzagging in poor visibility and depressing because we were getting

76

down towards the Cape so quickly, yet knowing that we had to turn back.

News today that America is turning the staffs of all the German Consulates out bears out my wishful thinking about the books coming into force today – ciphers etc. for British-USA intercommunication. There must surely be something definite about it or that the American fleet, for we have had the secret envelopes on board three months now. Why should they suddenly decide on a definite date otherwise? And in any case it seems almost as good as a declaration of war to turn out German Consulates. We are so short of news here and only have the *Edinburgh Castle* press to look forward to.

*Scythia* has evidently sailed for Gib with *Dunoon* but now there are orders that they are both to return unless *Dunoon* has sufficient fuel to go the whole way. Let us hope she hasn't, and then perhaps we might get the job of convoying her, which would be good fun and would probably give us a short holiday in Gib where I might see John Vulliamy. But that again is wishful thinking, I fear.

17 June 1941 – It's raining tonight, almost like the Western Approaches and amusingly a signal has come through to three old friends – *Wyvern*, *Wild* Swan and *Vansittart* – who are coming to Freetown for escort work.

Energetically cleared all the top drawer of my desk this afternoon, coming across old letters mixed up with the chocolate and cockroaches. That was depressing and I did my best not to read them. I read a recent one of Peter's though in which he writes of the incompetences and inadequacy of the infantry subaltern, who has to go out and command thirty men. Peter remarks that they probably know less than I did when I joined *Clematis*. I wonder if he realizes that I was responsible for sixty men and a ship at once and had no NCO's or anyone to whom I could turn for emergency decisions.

Bernard Shaw: Back to Methuselah: 'I had patience with them for many ages: they tried me very sorely. They did terrible things: they embraced death, and said that eternal life was a fable. I stood amazed at the malice and destructiveness of the things I had made: Mars blushed as he looked down on the shame of his sister planet: cruelty and hypocrisy become so hideous that the face of the earth was pitted with the graves of little children among which living skeletons crawled in search of horrible food.' (Lilith in last speech).

77

<u>20 June 1941</u> – 0900. There seems to have been a certain lack of grip lately, promoted as usual by the apathetic state of mind produced by the first few days in Freetown. There have been all the inevitable wasted evenings. Peter Castle has arrived in *Dunottar Castle* and Paul Giles in *Birmingham*, by whom John and I were invited to dinner last night with Peter Castle. We had had an extravagant afternoon, taking a taxi to Lumley and then up to Hill Station where we tried to play snooker but had to give the table up to Army officers when we realized that we would probably be anything up to an hour finishing, being quite unable to pot the yellow. Dinner was amusing, though too much was drunk and P.C. violently sick. Giles is quite unusual and has amusingly a complete ineptitude for all things naval.

<u>21 June 1941</u> – Germany has gone to war with Russia, which says a good deal for our Secret Service. It seems impossible not to forecast what will happen, but at least it must be certain that they will push the Russians back. Anyhow everyone is very excited at what is considered good news.

<u>23 June 1941</u> – Dinner and film with Peter Castle in *Dunottar Castle* tonight. Met a mysterious DF chap there who has apparently been living in the lighthouse for the last year who says there is a sailing boat we can have on the beach there. Peter and I are going to explore tomorrow.

<u>24 June 1941</u> – An amusing and original afternoon. I had arranged to meet P.C. but he didn't turn up so that I was eventually reduced to getting a taxi all to myself to the lighthouse. On the way I picked up No.1 and No.1 of *Cyclamen* but they left me, taking the taxi back again – I feeling completely lost and a little apprehensive as to how I was to get back, whether by boat or walking back to catch *Vindictive*'s boat. And anyhow I still had to find <u>the</u> boat. It was lying pulled up on the sand in a delightful bay, amongst the rocks. After surprisingly little persuasion I got the natives to help me pull it down to the water and to fetch the sails etc. But, as I had feared, it had been in the sun too long and leaked like a sieve, so that evening, with the help of the two empty peach tins, I didn't trust myself to get through the boom and to *Clematis*, as I would much like to have done. The natives though had obviously seen a chance to make some money and one suggested that he could repair and paint it but I would have to

78

provide the materials (which I intend to get free from the ship). It's not a good boat but playing about with it in that deserted bay I did forget about Freetown and all that Freetown means. And then I had a fine walk back along the beach for four miles, bathing on the way.

25 June 1941 – Crisis today: circulating inter pipe was dropped overboard from *Edinburgh Castle*. Considerable panic while divers began search.

26 June 1941 – Divers still searching – without success. Ashore but prevented from getting to Lumley by acute shortage of petrol, which even Annie Taylor can't get. Instead walked, with R. and Peter Castle, intending to bathe at the club and then go on further. But key to the swimming bath couldn't be found, so we just walked in the pouring rain. It was exceedingly pleasant though and I collected a very fine bunch of flowers.

27 June 1941 – After a hectic morning (the engines still aren't recovered) trying to get three and a half inch bolts and get the boat ready for sailing – went sailing with the Captain, J.F. and Reynolds for a bathe in a bay. The centreboard most surprisingly held and the boat sailed really well. The bathe too was a great success, in still warm, clear water, in peace – and now I have had a letter from home and Diana.

28 June 1941 – Still no sign of the pipe! Had hoped today to have a quiet sail by myself, but the Captain wanted to come and suggested bringing a few sailors and having a picnic which was, of course, a great suggestion. No sooner had we set out – with due ceremony – then it started to rain which it continued to do for the rest of the afternoon, harder and harder. I had rigged the jib and the main was fixed and the result was most encouraging. We seemed to slip along very well and sailed, if anything, closer to the wind. But we had decided to run back if it was still raining when we got to the bay – by which time we were all quite wet through. The Captain was still good tempered and I felt very happy, reminded vividly of so many other days sailing in Falmouth for instance. And then when we got back, by then distinctly cold, I had the delightful sensation of a hot wash and gradually getting warm afterwards. And in the evening we celebrated on the newly acquired red wine – of which now we have the full forty-four gallons.

But that night I dreamed very vividly and felt miserable in the morning at finding none of it there and myself still doing the same old job.

1 July 1941 – Still here – engines still being repaired, but they have started to make a spare part, which will be ready by Sunday. And over all there is mystery – caused by many rumours of convoys sailing to strange destinations at strange times and Naval Control Service staffs moving. In fact there is obviously a strong possibility that we may move across to Trinidad. Lately there have been very few ships in here (the last convoy was only nine and this one will be only ten). The funny thing is the Captain thinks we know all about it and tells John and me to keep it 'under our hats', but actually we know nothing. He says mysteriously that he supposes they will come back when this business is over – unless they are going to try for Dakar.

This might be a rest for us were there not the inevitable *Clematis* atmosphere which insists that we must pretend to be doing something whether one has anything to do or not. My mental state is getting worse too: it is almost agony for me to sit for any time at meals, knowing perfectly what anyone is going to answer to any given question. And visions of peace, and peaceful pursuits, seem to be slipping further and further away. The illustration for the calendar 'On the Warwickshire Avon' does not seem real even any longer.

Yet if only the Russians can keep their end up the war will be over quite soon. It doesn't look as if they can though.

2 July 1941 – A good afternoon, I remember, during which I left the Captain and strolled along the beach by myself towards the creek, wrote a letter to Diana, slept, bathed and just thought.

3 July 1941 – Convoy sailed today leaving no MV in the harbour except those unloading cargo or oilers. Everything very mysterious in fact but I see no signs of anything happening officially and begin to suspect that it may well be merely rumour promoted by a few coincidences.

4 July 1941 – I have been trying to get things organized for a little peace these last few days and, to that purpose, went for a long and strenuous walk up to Hill Station this afternoon by myself. Beforehand I found Friedmann whom Gwen had told me to call on: he looked as much like a German spy as his name suggests but he is

80

undoubtedly a great asset with his Wednesday afternoon tennis parties to which he invites *Oxfordshire* and others. Then the walk – it was strenuous but I kept going determinedly, perhaps encouraged by the thought of a glass of beer or lemon squash at the Club, and did it in about an hour and a quarter. It was fine to be by myself again and after the rains the grass had all come up, making it look more like England than ever. I felt homesick but even that was strangely pleasant, being able to feel homesick on my own, unworried by the others and knowing that they couldn't worry me until I decided to go back. But the bar was shut and all I could drink was water: it was misty and the Club was deserted. Yet the atmosphere should have been just what I wanted. I was tired and restless though and could hardly settle down to read illustrated papers even. Eventually I went to sleep for half an hour but when I woke up I realized how impossible it will be ever to get my peace of mind until this business is over. I so long (I realize that everyone else must be just the same) to be able to do what I like when I like and to be independent. It may be childish.

5 July 1941 – We had a fearsome game of hockey against *Vindictive* in the afternoon and had some of them to a celebration supper in the evening. The hockey was a good change but intolerably exhausting. I was playing right half where apparently I distinguished myself. Anyhow we only lost 1 – 0 and that in the last five minutes. In the evening Greenfield, Diggles, R. Forte, Litchfield and the Padre came to supper – and old Burgess, the RNVR engineer, was there too. They kept their promise and came in fancy dress – Diggles dressed as a Spanish Caballero with a magnificent wide brimmed hat and burnt cork beard and moustache, Greenfield a Chelsea artist in a brick coloured pyjama top and flowing yellow cloak (he looked the part perfectly with his own ginger beard), Forte, perhaps Little Lord Fauntleroy with beard and moustache (he hardly needed fancy dress) The supper was good and the drink worth it – the Cape white wine – none got drunk and everyone seemed happy. Yet surely the feature of the evening was R. Forte's native dance?

6 July 1941 – Arrived back from Lumley to find Cripps had arrived. I was feeling miserable as it was but seeing him made it far worse – poor chap he can't realize what he is in for at all. He was going to be an architect: he lives near Goring: he's quiet. I'm so sorry for the poor chap. Now I've had an old letter from Betty.

HMS Clematis
Wednesday 5th

Dear John.

We are to have our refit and reconstruction at Devonport on November 16th. Just the kind of news I always wish to receive whilst on leave!.

Yours
Staff

Cripps, inevitably known by us all as Stafford, or rather Staffy, was a great asset to the ship's company. As well as being an architect, he was a talented painter. Very typically it was he who took the trouble to write the letter above, knowing the feeling of disappointment as the end of ones leave approaches, on that occasion when we were in for a boiler clean after we had finally returned home to Liverpool. Very sadly he died not long after the war.

7 July 1941 – A day I shan't forget – Cripps having arrived, No.1 has calculated things well and gone sick: then, when everyone thought they had a few more days before going to sea, we had a signal saying we shall probably be needed early tomorrow.

8 July 1941 – We were needed and sailed with *Woodruff* and *Mignonette* at 0645. We had to oil first, leaving *Vindictive* at 0545 which was a dreadful strain, made doubly bad by No.1's absence, who was hurriedly taken across to *Oxfordshire* in the evening with a light attack of malaria. I dreaded this day. In the evening Philip Forte

invited me to hear some of his records after dinner, which I did, but only for half an hour. It had been a very busy day, doing No.1's job inspecting the decks all day and generally getting the ship ready for sea, hoisting boats etc; so that I was tired when I went across and considerably moved at hearing many of the records which I had heard M and Peter play so often – 'Jesu joy of man's desiring', for instance. For half an hour I forgot about the ship and the morrow but it couldn't last. Here I am therefore struggling to do this job as well as possible, wondering what the reaction of the men is and will be. So far it seems to be good, everyone having been very helpful and, I suspect, anxious to show that they will do their jobs without being harassed by No.1's worrying methods. But I am aware of the danger of being too easygoing. Anyhow, of course, it's by no means certain that No.1 will go – at least at once. Now though I hope he does for I should like to see how I can do the job and how the men will react.

Cripps has rather complicated things by going down with malaria himself, and badly.

9 July 1941 – Poor chap; I can imagine little worse than having malaria in a strange ship with strange people and a temperature – so far – of 102.5. He's a charming fellow too and obviously anxious to help. The result is John and I are doing all the worst watches, Lecky the forenoon and first.

It is a strange situation altogether; the whole atmosphere is strange, particularly at this time of night – eight – when I have the middle watch to come. There is so much that may happen, even running into a Vichy ship, and so much that may go wrong. Yet there is something so relentless about it that I feel inevitably we shall do our patrol, meet the two oil tankers, return to Freetown, get our mail and be ready to come out again on the same old job all over again. Yes, there is always so much that might happen; perhaps in a year – as I have said and thought so often there will be no ship to worry about and instead I shall be sitting in a comfortable room about to get into a comfortable bed, knowing that I shall not have to get up at midnight.

10 July 1941 – Fortunately nothing has happened but life is very busy in three watches again – and never the long sleep – and looking after the ship as well. This morning the Captain inspected the mess decks after the great drive to get bunks and lockers clean. They looked quite surprisingly clean, far better than I have ever seen them before, with

all the bunks properly made. It seemed that they really had made an effort, as indeed, miraculously, everyone seems to have done; they seem all to be going out of their way, as it were, to help – Sewell especially obviously trying hard and apparently as anxious as I am to make a success of it.

Cronin's *Grand Canary* isn't up to much – seems poorly written too. Hear Free French have asked for armistice in Syria and that Americans, having occupied Iceland, swear they will sink any Germans who try to interfere.

Vague raider reports round four degrees North; hope there is nothing in them for it is just where we are.

12 July 1941 – Now everything has gone wrong. This morning No.1 came back with great flourish and announced that he hoped to sail in *Abasso* on Tuesday. I hoped he would; I had become interested and keen on the job and, having started it, hate having to hand it over to him again. But the Captain wouldn't let him go and seemed unreasonable about the whole thing. It thoroughly depressed and annoyed me – faced with returning to all the old routine and all the old quarrels, besides which there will now be six of us to do the quarrelling and four to sleep in two bunks. It is unfortunate that in wartime we manage to get the small things so much out of proportion and forget about the big things.

15 July 1941 – Out on the interminable eight-day convoy this morning – all six of us. It should be a luxury trip for Cripps and Lecky are keeping the day watches and we are changing round on the night ones. I should have plenty of time to read a bit and sleep. Indeed I think the trouble may be too much sleep and too much to eat. News is scarce and I have done nothing enterprising, except play hockey again yesterday against *Vindictive*. Again we lost 1 – 0 and again it was almost indescribably exhausting, besides which I had made the fatal mistake of having a mug of lemonade before it started with the result that from half time onwards I felt absolutely sick and eventually had to change places for a rest. But it was great fun and I look forward to playing again. We had hoped for a lot of mail but very little came and we are still missing from 5 – 19th. There was a fine letter from D, showing again the undisturbed morale of the people at home, so much better than most of us. The only war news is that it has been definitely established that we are out here for eighteen

84

1. The Author.

2. HMS *Clematis*.

3. A signalman on board *Clematis*, 1940.

4. Leading Seaman Reynolds, *Clematis*.

5. *Clematis* attacking the *Hipper* on Christmas Day, 1940 and making smoke to conceal the convoy.

6. An unusually calm sea in the Atlantic, en route for Gibraltar.

7. The open bridge of *Clematis*. The first on the left is the author's brother-in-law, John Ellyatt.

8. A River Class frigate, sister ship to HMS *Exe*.

9. The ship's cat in *Exe*.

10. *Exe* oiling at sea – always a difficult business.

11. Transferring the writer Alan Moorhead from *Exe* just before a near disaster. Moorhead is second from the left.

12. Members of the course at HMS *Dryad*, 1943. The author is seated, extreme right.

13. HMS *Amethyst*.

14. *Amethyst's* officers; author standing second from right.

15. Leading Wren Mary Ellyatt, later to become a Petty Officer and the author's wife.

16. The author with his brother-in-law to be on the morning of the wedding, having had a drink.

17. The wedding, February 1945.

18. Reunion after fifty years (see Chapter XII).

months. Yet I have almost trained myself to stop thinking of the future now – and even the present. As I wrote home my values have changed. So many things, which I used to think important, are trivial now. If only we can all have the chance to put our new ideas to the test.

16 July 1941 – It is quite a lovely scene with the cat asleep on the floor of the cabin by my bunk. In fact this cabin is almost civilized now were it not so hot and stuffy and infested with cockroaches. But I feel everything is too easy and life too peaceful to last. Cripps is a great asset and obviously has a good grip. An interruption whilst I got a drink for the cat, in the lid of the hot water can. But after it had only drunk very little it spotted a cockroach and adjourned to play with it and then eat it. If it could only catch this one remaining rat which, it is reported, the other night jumped into Major East's hammock!

18 July 1941 – It is now definitely established that I am not the type to win the war, having just had the monthly row with the Captain about Jews. I could write a lot about it – all the usual arguments – but now the cat has become restless and by means of one of my drawers has jumped on to the table by my bunk, obviously after the rat, which has its hole immediately over my head through in to the stokers' mess. It is a truly terrifying spectacle; it is indeed bad enough to have the rat without the added complication of a cat with the possibility that no sooner have I got to sleep then the thing will crawl on me and scare me out of my wits. Animals in fact are getting on my nerves and not only live ones. Last night I had a horribly realistic dream that my wooden vulture had come to life and was sitting on my bunk, looking at me, hypnotising me. At first when I woke up all I was conscious of was the memory of this horrible bird and I couldn't remember what connection it had with my life, until I saw the old wooden vulture peering down at me.

Tonight I have the middle. Time is passing more quickly than usual and with the day off I have even had time to read a bit. But I can't settle down and certainly of course periodic contact flaps aren't conducive to peaceful thinking. I had only just announced at lunch time that I was going to spend the afternoon as though I were on a £100 cruise when *Woodruff* got a contact and dropped a depth charge, causing the usual disturbance. It is strange to think that there might have been something there and that sixty men might have been killed on that peaceful summer day.

<u>19 July 1941</u> – Japan will soon have joined us all it seems. The Government having resigned, they are now behaving threateningly towards Russia and we have started to talk about Singapore and – apparently – have even sent some reserve pilots out there. Of course it will finish the Russians completely unless then Americans help them – and I imagine we shall very soon lose the Gilbert and Ellice and Solomon Isles. The Captain will complain that it is yet another example of the result of tolerance. For he would not be tolerant (and indeed he isn't) and would not accept it as being a component of freedom. Nor – I am still harping back to last night – will he admit that the forceful expulsion of Jews from Germany is a contradiction of freedom, but would have us do the same and claims failure to do so being the cause of our troubles. Arguing with him almost convinces me that I am fighting for basic principles and not just my own skin. Perhaps it is a form of inferiority complex but I don't consider my own skin to be worth anything unless it be surrounded by an atmosphere which can inspire it to something more than mere animal interests.

<u>21 July 1941</u> – It has been very civilized this trip, having all day free. But it is fatal so far as relaxing in the wardroom is concerned and I really don't see how it can possibly go on for another year. Perhaps it is just because I now find most meals agony, watching every movement of the Captain, No.1 and Lecky and unable to speak unless it be to argue. I'm afraid there really is bitterness now too.

The Captain has decided that we are in the midst of hordes of U-boats, having had signals to alter course to avoid suspected ones and having picked up a signal from the Admiralty to *Moreton Bay* saying that a dummy distress message has been picked up in our area. He now sleeps on the bridge and mutters periodically that we shall see something of the war in the next two days and making an order that the men should wear their lifebelts after dark. But we have only one more night left; then we go straight back to Freetown and *Woodruff* and *Mignonette* to Bathurst for the eighty survivors.

I have amazed myself during the last two mornings, fixing the bracket for the mast on the thwart of one of the lifeboats which, in spite of all my efforts, looks very jerry-built. The wood was too hard and the screws too soft with the result that even with the help of a hatchet as a hammer I have been unable to get the screws in properly. It is all singularly trivial but it amuses me.

23 July 1941 – We left the convoy this evening at six after a great interchange of signals with *Moreton Bay*, it all resulting in *Woodruff* and *Mignonette* having to stay an extra night, they being the two detailed for the survivors from Bathurst. They must have been furious – eight days is long enough and besides *Mignonette* can only do ten knots, probably after losing the convoy and doing full speed for too long in a vain attempt to catch up without being noticed. It was early morning and when light broke there was no sign of her, nor had *Cyclamen* seen her. But ten minutes later *Cyclamen* reported ship bearing 180, presumably corvette; at the same time we intercepted Cape Sable, signalling that ship appeared to be corvette. It was hardly surprising. It had been a very dark night – now that there is no moon. It struck me as rather a striking sight when we left and a perfect propaganda photograph – a convoy of thirty loaded ships, led by the AMC, 'standing out against the Eastern sky', strangely enough the sister ship of *Jervis Bay*. There certainly was something very striking about it and I couldn't help wondering how many of them would be lost on the way home, for some of them are almost bound to be. Which? *Belgravian* was there and we wished her good luck. Certainly the Captain deserves it after his effort in the famous S.L. convoy. Now I wonder if this peaceful trip can last; the Action Bell hasn't been rung at all yet and we have had every day free. I feel a little refreshed and would be much more so were it not for the intolerable atmosphere.

24 July 1941 – What are the Japanese going to do? They are now said to have seven battleships and thirty destroyers waiting for Indo China so there was little else we could do other than gracefully say 'we were ready for them'. The Lieutenant Commander who came aboard who had just come from Hong Kong said that the China fleet now only consisted of two out of date cruisers, two old destroyers, a sloop or two and some gunboats. Yet I do for once feel confident that we can deal with the Japs all right – given the chance. It has always been said that their ships are the same quality as their toys.

26 July 1941 – It was a bad day today, ending even more badly than it began. It started with *Cyclamen* bearings running in the morning watch, causing us to remain stopped until noon and then proceed at slow speed and ended with the Action Bell at 9.30 and a terrific cockroach appeared afterwards. It was my night off but by the time it came to turn in I had even seen the rat as well. The Action was a strange

business. Without warning the SO reported hydrophone effect of a fast moving engine on the port side and then the firing of a torpedo. We did all we could – at least we missed the torpedo if there was one – and searched for some time but could find nothing. (In the middle of it all *Cyclamen* piped up about his old bearings.) Yes, it was a bad evening for me. I was very apprehensive aft. It isn't easy to get a grip quickly when you can't see anything and yet there is always the probability that we will fire the first depth charge quickly, which would mean reloading in a hurry. It always seems to work out all right in the end but I know that once things started to go wrong they would never get right again.

But the cockroach hunt is perhaps even worse. They are becoming quite intolerable down here, particularly in No.1's cabin – crawling all over the bulkheads and even in his bunk. All we can do is to fumigate it but I don't suppose we ever shall.

**It is a strange reflection that anxiety about rats and cockroaches should, it seems, be greater than about U-boats and raiders.**

27 July 1941 – Now we have left *Cyclamen* and are going on on our own. We should be in by noon tomorrow – the worst possible time because it will mean endless panic with oilers and water boats. But still we shall get letters and perhaps news from the Admiralty or C-in-C.

28 July 1941 – In at 1030 this morning, making a bad landfall too far to the southward, seeing land quite suddenly. The old tense atmosphere started almost at once. But I had a very pleasant afternoon, sailing with Palmer of *Columbine* down to the bay by the lighthouse, there having most peaceful bathing. As soon as we came round the stern of *Edinburgh Castle*, I saw him rigging their boat and at once saw a chance to avoid other plans such as a run ashore, which I did not fancy. As it was I much enjoyed myself and felt pleasantly detached during dinner, the more so because there had been a mail with a box of chocolates and letters from home and a book from Diana (Kipling – *Actions and Reactions*). There is as yet no news of anyone going or indeed of anything and hardly any Freetown gossip – except a signal from *Asphodel*. There are no rumours yet as to how long we shall be in, but a convoy will be sailing at the weekend so presumably we shall go with it – inevitably.

There follow in the next few entries some irrelevant entries which had no connection with the war but perhaps illustrate the thoughts which passed through the mind of a young sailor who, one fears, was beginning to be in danger of reaching the end of his tether. If only to that extent it is interesting to read of what went through his mind.

29 July 1941 – This morning – Tuesday – my day on, it is pouring with rain and looks as if the two hundred inches have really started to fall at last. It is dark and grey more like the old Marlow, making me feel very homesick. But that is hardly constructive. Meanwhile the Russians are holding their own at least and Germany has been forced to appeal to Italy and Romania for help, which seems too good to be true. Japan, on the other hand, is doing what she likes with U.S.A. merely 'freezing credits' in reply. I am doing nothing. Quite un-expected orders that we would be wanted at 1800. At 1700 just as we were on our way to the oiler orders came that we are to escort convoy of six ships to Takoradi. They must have tried to keep it secret until the last moment and even in the orders it says that ships have the impression they are going to disperse. As we left it was very grim – pouring with rain, mail from home just aboard and John not with us for the first time; and I had an uncomfortable feeling, but I feel better now. It was striking sailing at that time. When we had left the tanker the rain had stopped, leaving a fine wild sunset against which the five ships were silhouetted as they went through the boom, and we went close enough to *Edinburgh Castle* for me to be able to see John had got a pair of glasses himself. We waved to each other. I wondered what he was feeling. He probably knew what I was. Then we caught the ships up, had a chat with the Commodore through the hailing gear, and are now stationed in our usual place. It is a clear moonlight night. It is a scene which would certainly strike people at home – the small convoy of valuable ships setting out on their last lap, presum-ably loaded with Hurricanes. Let's hope they will get there. Plenty might happen but it surely won't?

I have had some delightful letters and books from home. If only we didn't have to fight.

1 August 1941 – Quite a lot to write but no inclination to write it, brought about largely by Freetown rain, which is overbearingly oppressive. I think John's departure with a broken toe to *Oxfordshire* depressed and annoyed me too: he was having a race on Lumley Beach

when typically he fell, twisted and broke his big toe causing him to be discharged by *Edinburgh Castle* to *Oxfordshire* apparently for three weeks. However today I have, most sympathetically, been over to see him and discover that he is returning tomorrow in spite of toe (heroically, so I told the Captain for his benefit, rejoining his ship). Otherwise nothing of interest or excitement has happened: we just await orders, vaguely hoping that we may go to Lagos for the long-postponed docking. Yesterday we played hockey with newly bought hockey sticks against *Vindictive* and drew 1 – 1 – should have beaten them had they not scored in last five minutes. Tomorrow we play *Asphodel* and Monday *Milford* or *Cothay*. In the evening I had dinner in *Vindictive* with Greenfield and the others and saw some very fine photographs and slides – many of Lagos, which look typical and enticing. Otherwise nothing, not even new mail.

I have bought the only book in the Christian Mission Shop – Fowler's *Modern English Usage*.

3 August 1941 – It seems increasingly difficult to enjoy myself. I used to enjoy going for a bathe at Lumley but now I don't and even consider staying on board instead – perhaps it is because we are spoilt, for indeed we do spend longer in now. But I'm afraid it's not that. It is just a tired mental state.

Tonight I have been across to *Vindictive* to cold dinner with Forte and Cripps, which was peaceful and good, and have talked on many subjects from archaeology to the Eton Wall Game on which I imagine Philip could always be drawn.

Still there is no news of what we are to do, except that we shall definitely not be taking the convoy. It is an intolerable routine. I was thinking almost exactly the same thoughts four months ago. Life is standing still for me now it seems; it is no mere figure of speech.

5 August 1941 – 'Thank God that so hath blessed thee, and sit down Robin and rest thee'. Diana says that 'On Habitation Enforce' is her favourite short story – which is quite beside the point except that I don't really feel blessed at this moment, nor have I much chance to sit down and rest. The weather is poor with quite a strong head wind and sea and visibility is hopeless, causing No.1 to have to stay up until a quarter to five when I took over from him last night. There is no doubt we are all getting tired and stale now.

A magnificent supply of books, including *Of Human Bondage*

which seems admirably Maugham and detached. In fact I have a fine supply now and am educating myself a little for the first time.

The Captain tells of a prison camp, chiefly for Vichy French, inland from Freetown which is apparently thoroughly 'un-British' – chiefly because it is so unhealthy. No wonder the French are treating our chaps badly in Konakry. Will the Dusuzeaus ever talk to me again?

<u>6 August 1941</u> – Talking to Cripps this afternoon we agreed that the majority of people at home don't really know much about the war. I was started off by the letter from Diana, telling of her visit to Oxford and the almost perfect illusion they have been able to maintain there, apparently as many undergraduates as ever. Perhaps a year ago I would have thought nothing of it other than to say I thought it essential to continue 'civilised' life, but now it disturbs me considerably – disturb is not the right word – that anyone can leave school and spend anything up to a year and half there, completely regardless of the war. Are they being incredibly strong minded? Or is it just that they don't realize how damnable war is? Can they be the same type – as Diana suggests – who five years ago were thinking realistically about China and Spain and in some cases fighting? We are the ones who are wrong no doubt, but how futile it all seems to us, playing at being intellectual and getting a war degree. Isn't there so much more at stake? It is trite – but what good will their war degrees be if we lose this war.

We should get to Takoradi by Saturday evening or Sunday. With any luck there will be no ships ready to sail. We are past the danger zone now and should get there peacefully so long as we don't run into Vichy.

91

# CHAPTER VI

# Takoradi and Lagos

<u>7 August 1941</u> – It is in a way distressing to read *Of Human Bondage* now. Obviously it would be an excellent stimulant for the lazy mind, producing ideas which might even be put into practice, but now it only makes me more and more conscious of how hopelessly trapped I am and of what slight outlet there is for the energy of ambition.

<u>9 August 1941</u> – I'm sitting in the Captain's chair on the wing of the bridge outside Takoradi harbour. It has been a singularly unsuccessful day. After some anxiety due to thick rain which made an awkward landfall worse, we finally got into the harbour at eight, only to be told to go out again and screen the ships until pilots could take them in. It seemed very childish but there was no alternative so out we went again like naughty boys and anchored ourselves whilst *Crocus* patrolled. Then it was decided we could oil so in we went again, after great labours tied up to a wharf, but now have had to come out to relieve *Crocus* until 1800 when the ships go in. We have landed liberty men but only two officers, it eventually being decided that Cripps and Lecky should go in the afternoon. I had been looking forward to exploring a few shops but felt bound to stay. So here we are. Takoradi looks quite civilized and clean, even better than Bathurst, the harbour looking very like an English one and for the first time for six months we tied up to dry land. Naval Officer in Charge, a fussy Lieutenant Commander RN who must relive the chances of a good job, informs us that we shall sail tomorrow. He had said in the evening but then said it would be eight – which is a pity for I had looked forward to a complete night in and then a stroll ashore by myself.

At six we went in. Now I am alone on board. I just could not face going ashore with No.1 or Lecky which would just have meant tagging on, uninvited, to the RAF. No, I just couldn't face it, much as I would love to go ashore peacefully by myself even just to walk haphazardly. Instead I am staying aboard and the others have gone. It is so strange being tied up again: I have just been strolling up and down the quay. There is a gentle breeze blowing and the moon is just rising. You can hear the rumbling of the surf in the outer harbour quite clearly. In fact I am quite unable to explain my feelings as I stood on the quay looking at the old ship: she looked impressive and yet strangely friendly and I felt sentimental. I felt sorry too for the watch aboard who have missed the only chance of late leave they have had for seven months and sent the gramophone and two bottles of wine along. I shouldn't have done it – the wine I mean – but having once thought of it, had to. If only I could describe my feelings on these occasions or, so much better, the atmosphere when everything is unreal. Shall I still remember it in two years' time?

Vichy ships are laying mines now. RAF say that Vichy ship left Lagos and mines were found, then went to Takoradi and the same happened again.

10 August 1941 – We left at 5.30 this morning I felt very tired, more so than ever before, perhaps merely because of the rat which frightened me so badly before I turned in! I first spotted it over the stove in the wardroom and threw a shoe at it, but missed, frightening it into our cabin where I chased it behind the radiator. Yet it could certainly not have been as frightened as I was when, with a torch and another shoe, I looked for it. I couldn't find it – obviously because I was too tired to look properly for when I switched off the main light it scuttled out from precisely where I had pretended to look and ran across the pipes over my bunk again whilst I stood and watched it, petrified, unable to throw the shoe even.

**I seem to have been more frightened of a rat than a U-boat, of which there were still a lot in the area as well as German capital ships and Armed Merchant Cruisers.**

Now we are on our way back with two ships and should be in by Thursday evening. I am worried though because I find I am beginning to lose the ability to live from day to day, looking forward even to Freetown and reading little more than Weekly Intelligence Reports and magazines. Instead I dream of things to come in which I am encouraged by Cripps who, though he thinks more clearly, feels much the same. I asked Bowles this evening how he liked Takoradi (they all thoroughly enjoyed themselves) and he replied, 'It's all right, what I saw of it, but it's a long road back.'

Reminded of the *Voltaire* by the Weekly Intelligence Reports. She was presumably sunk by raider, unable even to send out report. It was just after the *Britannia*, only three or four hundred miles from Freetown.

11 August 1941 – Peace abruptly disturbed this evening. I had the last dog watch; it was much darker than usual and I had just got especially close to the Commodore for Cripps when he signalled quite casually, 'Small object passed port side, like sub.' Consequent pandemonium; I couldn't believe anything could have got between us and therefore didn't act very quickly; however, I was quicker than I expected to be, going hard a'port and full ahead. It was devilishly dark so that the Captain could see nothing for the first five minutes at least and I had an anxious time charging about whilst we got into RT touch with *Crocus* and fired starshell. To make matters worse we actually picked up a contact and passed over it. We fired five charges, causing some pandemonium as one got jammed. However, we gave satisfaction in the end, the charge not fortunately slipping out at slow speed of which I was apprehensive. Looking back I don't really see how there could have been anything there, but it was disturbing even so. Now we are just rejoining them again. At least we've got rid of five of the old rusty charges and Kent is pleased.

12 August 1941 – The night was peaceful after all but I am apprehensive there will be another panic this evening. There nearly was when, during dinner, the oil tanks rumbled so that it sounded like a depth charge. I was sorry to find I was quite nervous and excited. After dinner talk centred on raiders which is never exactly cheerful, the Captain grumbling at our AMCs and *Bonaventure* and *Berwick*. Certainly some Merchant Ships have fought magnificently – one for two and a half hours before she was sunk. There must be many stories of the twenty-one the *Scharnhorst* and *Gneisenau* sank.

13 August 1941 – Have just been reading the March A/S report. It would certainly wake up any civilian to read it and for that matter Army and Air Force. It is quite extraordinary what these merchant ships go through. Presumably though they don't realize the risks until it actually happens. HG53 for instance, escorted by *Velox* and *Deptford* – they were first attacked a day or two after leaving Gib when three or four ships were sunk. Neither of the escorts could do anything about it with a force which in any case was quite inadequate. It was repeated the next night when about four more went, including the Commodore. Again, in the general pandemonium, all the escorts could do was to pick up survivors (in one case a ship which the night before had picked up thirty-one from a torpedoed ship was herself sunk and there was only one survivor from the whole lot). Still they carried on, only to be then picked up by a Focke-Wulf who got four more. Finally it is now reported that it is believed *Hipper* was told their position and instructed to intercept; she found SL64 instead and sunk seven of them. There are hundreds of other stories – the Bermuda section of the HX convoy now have to go independently to Halifax because of surface raiders; at least a whole convoy can't get sunk then. Yet, in spite of all that, we are getting the upper hand. We have, after all, accounted now for all the aces, including Prien (one of the well-known U-boat commanders) and in an attack on the HX convoy three were destroyed.

We get in at 1500 tomorrow so I only have one more watch – four to eight. Although we have been doing it for over a year now and are likely to for many more, I still think of the last watch of a trip with relief.

**We had again been lucky not to have been involved as we so easily might have been. It was strange at one moment to be in danger of being sunk and the next to be playing hockey as we did the next day**

14 August 1941 – In and John back plus mail. He had obviously benefited from the rest and looked fatter than ever. I felt thoroughly depressed – no news and everything exactly the same as ever.

15 August 1941 – Cheered up today by good game of hockey with *Eagle*. We had intended to play *Vindictive* but they were engaged so we courageously challenged *Eagle*. At short notice they very

sportingly accepted and turned out a very pleasant team – nearly all officers. They beat us 4 – 0 but it was a much closer game than the score suggests, especially as one was offside. We did well since they have never been beaten in two and a half year's commission. Then they came off for a drink – considerable – and invited us over in the evening to flicks and supper which was very sporting of them. It was civilized and enjoyable, and impressive – that is the calm cheerfulness of men who have been through hell at Tobruk and Benghazi as well as all over the Med (Taranto) and almost everywhere else as well. Many of them had decorations. What is more they have done more sea time than any other ship. The Captain is annoyed. The new Captain D has arrived but is presumably responsible for order that destroyers shall be Senior Officer, which caused the Captain to tell me 'confidentially' that he proposed handing in his resignation. But it looks as if they have got round it all by putting ourselves and *Asphodel* as spare members of the striking force and special force. It may be better and should mean any good jobs going.

20 August 1941 – We should have played hockey again against *Eagle* but grounds were unfit for play. It has rained almost continually now for three days so that I shall be glad when we go out tomorrow. It is the Westerly Southbound, which came in on the eighteenth. I saw them come in and was most depressed by it – about fifteen troopers, all nearly as big as the *Britannic*, packed tight with troops, so tight that an individual stood for nothing. Yet I suppose if any one of those troopships could be reproduced again with the same troops in six months time there would be big hard gaps along the decks. No one seems interested in what the ships contain at all – a convoy is just a collection of so many ships, not of so many thousand human men, with friends and homes. They are trite things to say but nearly everything in war is.

21 August 1941 – Out with this enormous convoy. I suppose there must be at least fifty thousand troops, yet there are only four of us, *Jupiter* and *Edinburgh*. Reading the W.I.Rs which become more interesting about Vichy France and their incredible attitude; the concentration camp at Konakry for instance seems as bad as anything in Germany – hopelessly foul conditions, dirt and fever, and intolerable treatment. But apparently it is only the police who are responsible for it. The civilians and doctors do their best, which suggests it is run

by Germans. Amongst others the crew of *Criton* are there. It's an extraordinarily tragic story.

But the account of the escape of the Norwegian ship from Dakar is fine – of how they made duplicate parts for the engine and exchanged them for the real ones after they persuaded the French to let them carry out trials, of how they broke through the boom and escaped the patrols.

Surface raiders are about again. On 30th a ship was sunk in 16N 38W and now another one.

<u>22 August 1941</u> – Panic this evening about U-boats – reported ship torpedoed in 5N, a position we were due to pass through nearby. It must have disturbed them a bit in C-in-C's office to think of eighteen big troopships escorted by only four corvettes and one destroyer. There would be the most ghastly confusion if anything were to happen. Confusion is bad enough already on *Clematis* bridge without that. It was bad down here too after dinner – John had just turned in and I was sitting talking to him when the rat appeared from behind the radiator; we both screamed and dashed out into the wardroom to find a severe smell of burning which caused yet more confusion. People rushed for fire buckets, shouted for keys to stores, and in a few minutes the wardroom was invaded by stand-by men with fire buckets. But meanwhile Cripps and I, braving the fearful gases, had opened the store, discovered it not to be the seat of the fire and traced it to the refrigerator. I would have sent for the whole ship's company before thinking of switching it off, but Cripps was very prompt and the fire was stopped.

<u>24 August 1941</u> – Left this morning whilst I slept peacefully. It is always pleasant to get up in the morning to find us on our own again. It was a relief that nothing happened too.

Wrote to Gwen this morning – 'Shall one be expected to behave after the war as, we are told, our fathers did after the last? Shall we be expected either to settle down to a sound job and family life or live in drink and sin? Shan't we be able just to drift abroad and wander haphazardly from country to country, meeting friends when we want to, disappearing when we want to, returning sentimentally when we want to? Or will our friends say of us "poor chap, it's the reaction after the war you know; he's never settled down"? But even if they say it of us we shall know they are wrong. We shall remember those days when our only ambition was to be free and we shall look on their patronising criticism with tolerant amusement. Perhaps we shall even remember the crabs doing their physical jerks on the sand at False Cape. They will still be doing them then with the same complete detachment.

'I can hear the same old records being played in the wardroom next door. They produce a most extraordinary atmosphere and I know that twenty years hence they would still produce it – remind me now of Rosyth, Liverpool (and all that they stood for), a few peacetime dances very vaguely; and reminding us then – twenty years hence – of all that mixed together, that life of endless worries and fears, endless disappointments and false hopes.'

25 August 1941 – Spent this morning and the first dog at manoeuvres, all of which were badly executed but passed the time quickly – only one more watch, 10 – 12: tomorrow we are in, except for the unfortunate *Anchusa* who had been detached to meet a ship in 2N.

I have now taken to making full use of the deck chairs, this afternoon particularly when I read and slept very comfortably until three. There is something pleasantly friendly about a deck chair. *Revenge* is on her way down.

26 August 1941 – Just when we thought we were getting in we had orders to meet WS 10X – five ships, *Dorsetshire, Brilliant, Velox* and *Wrestler. Cyclamen* had broken down again and *Anchusa* had already gone down to the other ship to the south, so *Crocus* and ourselves had to go. It was a bad evening. I had just come on watch at 2215 when I became conscious of what looked like a white horse ahead and simultaneously realized that there wasn't enough wind for a white horse. It was a ship coming straight for us, fast and close. We both just altered to starboard and missed, challenging him at the same time. At first I thought it was an M.V. but she answered with pendants 68. That was *Wishart*, but *Wishart* shouldn't be in these parts and in any case the Anti-Submarine operator gave it as reciprocating engines. Hence mystery and much dramatization by the Captain who, after having been convinced that it wasn't a U-boat, had wild ideas that it might be an enemy destroyer making a dash for it, though God knows where from or to.

My diary does not solve the mystery and I am afraid I do not remember it.

There was a signal during the day from Admiralty that German U-boats are using RT PL to give phoney messages to escorts, which is interesting after the noises we heard on the RT the last night with the convoy.

27 August 1941 – We met WS 10X dead ahead this morning and have since been wondering whether we shall manage to keep up, their signalled speed being fourteen and a half knots. In the news last night it was announced that *Picotex* and seven MVs had been lost off Portugal. It is extraordinary after all the rumours about her being lost during the last six months which had been proved false. Yet she really has gone – the first known to be lost by enemy action.

**I am afraid the rather odd name means nothing to me.**

Wrote to Betty – '*Clematis* has steamed fifty thousand miles in just over a year and I'm afraid it looks as if we may steam another fifty thousand before I get back to England, but now, shut away in this small ship, thrown together with people I have not chosen for my friends, I am constantly filled with dreadful ambitions, longing to be free again – to be able to live again with friends, to be able to travel where I want (I long for that more than anything). Frustration is making me bitter and unreasonably bad tempered with my fellows. I used to have limitless faith in human nature, was ashamed of myself when I was so frequently selfish and mean, but now that all seems tragically to have changed. I had not realized, I suppose, how lucky I was in my friends so that, spoiled by them then, I feel it so much the more now. It is only the expression of temporary depression, brought on by the constant grind of this tiring war in which individual effort seems to play such a desperately small part.'

28 August 1941 – Laval has been shot, spreading Anti Communism in Paris; assassin was arrested but crowd nearly lynched police. Darlan has more power than ever; we are doing well in Iran; Russians still holding them up.

30 August 1941 – It all started on Sunday when Captain D came aboard; from that moment there has been no peace. That evening No.1 went and I was left in charge and the following day C-in-C

signalled that he might come to have a look at accommodation, which he did at noon and stayed for half an hour. When he went round the mess decks they were all at lunch, but sitting down incredibly tidily like small boys on a Sunday School treat. The atmosphere was tense but when he made as if to say something it became unbearably so. Perhaps they expected him to say they were now going home. All he did say was – 'We all know you are living an uncomfortable life but you have the consolation of knowing that we appreciate what a damned fine job you are doing.' I felt everyone man there was bitterly disappointed.

Then that evening a great exchange of signals began as to our possible accommodation, Captain D doing his best throughout to persuade C-in-C that there wasn't any. It ended badly.

2 September 1941 – An immense amount has happened and I feel very tired and very lonely. We got in from the WS 10X, heard many more rumours than usual, ending in No.1 going, the ship going to Lagos for quick docking and our taking for passage – two Free French officers, five Army officers, one civilian and fifteen ratings. It has been the most tiring day of all, added to by my having a cold.

3 September 1941 – It's getting a bit better now and is becoming rather amusing – particularly the two Frenchmen. They were really the only ones to survive, the Army being completely under the weather. I think they must toss up each day to who is to keep up their reputation and appear for meals, for there is seldom more than one there now and he invariably disappears very hurriedly towards the end. Yet it is not rough at all. I realize it is not surprising, that I used to feel the motion. However, it eases matters considerably; congestion will become acute if they all recover.

4 September 1941 – I suppose it is that I had got so used to the old routine that anything new is bound to be tiring. Certainly, though, this is – intensely. And the trouble is I fear it may be no better the other end. At Lagos we are bound, I fear, to be pestered with trivial necessities, not to be mention in my case worrying about all the repairs. There is something disturbing about having the two Frenchmen too. They are so lost in this environment and the Captain behaves so atrociously to them, particularly tonight for instance when he allowed the steward to serve us before them. In fact this ship is the

base of so many conflicting emotions just now that I feel more on edge than I have done for many months.

5 September 1941 – Tomorrow the convoy splits up – the Cape portion dispersing, Takoradi with *Bridgwater* and *Asphodel* and ourselves. We were disturbed last night by *Asphodel* imagining she had a contact and firing Very lights and starshell but nothing came of it except excitement for the Army. The novelty of being No.1 is pleasant as yet and the crew seem disposed to be as helpful as they can.

Germans still driven back from Leningrad and the first encounter between U.S. naval patrols and Germans – a U-boat apparently trying to sink an American destroyer.

The Free Frenchmen argue in favour of the metric system and play bridge most keenly – tonight with the Captain. The Capitaine de frigate is for Alexandria and the Colonel for Syria.

6 September 1941 – The two Frenchmen become more amusing. Tonight they have had more wine than usual so that when the good old argument about ideals and the shirt on one's back started I was most apprehensive. It was tragic that the old Colonel said he was fighting for the shirt on his back and not for Fraternité, Liberté, Egalité. Fortunately it didn't quite develop into a heated argument although the Captain did his best to make it, in his complete inability to realize that anyone can argue purely for a certain viewpoint without necessarily believing in it oneself. The Army fellow was claiming that, even though it may have been misguided the Government had a policy during the two years before the war, to turn Russia and Germany against each other and that they had therefore made a mistake in supporting Franco in Spain. The ship runs smoothly and I am still keen.

8 September 1941 – Arrived Lagos noon today. We should have been in very much earlier but *Atlantic Coast* slowed up for two hours during the night putting us twenty mils astern and then it was a dark misty morning so that we had considerable panic even finding the place. And when we did they wouldn't let us in. The day before there had been a mild flap too when we intercepted a fairly large passenger ship which looked as if it might be Vichy. Boarding parties etc. were got ready (including one of the Army) and I had horrible visions of

sailing the thing in to Lagos. But fortunately not. Now we are tied up alongside *Atlantic Coast* in mid-stream. Nothing has been done about refit and there is no news even of getting into dock. In fact it is the anti-climax we expected and I am most apprehensive. Perhaps if we live ashore it can't be so bad but even that is by no means definite. Why on earth can't the local residents do something for us?

9 September 1941 – We shipped to a berth alongside this afternoon and are now much better off. Tonight the sailors have had night leave for the first time for nine months but now – midnight – only ten are still ashore. Of course there just isn't anywhere for the decent ones to go. But I shall certainly be extravagant and spend one night at the Grand if I can. Lieutenant Commander (E) came aboard and was thoroughly pessimistic about repairs and indeed it doesn't look as if much will be done.

But it looks as if we might enjoy ourselves. Palmer, my namesake and pre-war friend, came across this evening and chatted very pleasantly amongst other things of Lagos amusements. I shall see. It will largely depend on whether I can get ashore by myself in the afternoon to wander round, I think, and that seems doubtful.

News still promising – landing on Spitzbergen and Germans still being driven back from Smolensk. What price I wonder?

The others ashore this evening to dinner with Army and Free Frenchmen at Grand which was apparently good. French pilot there, who had escaped from Syria, crashed and lived wild with the natives for weeks.

10 September 1941 – What an incredible life it is. It seemed stranger than ever before, driving back this evening from Lagos through what seemed by moonlight typical English country. But everything is so different from that. After a pleasant evening with the Captain and John during which we had a good dinner at the Grand (the best but thoroughly poor).

11 September 1941 – We went up to the Golf Club this afternoon, played golf, most erratically in my case, sat outside drinking lemon squash, had a shower, dinner and then dancing. It was all most civilized and for some reason depressing. We were lucky after dinner to be introduced to an Army Sister, having a dance each with her, strictly in turn. She was sophisticated and intelligent and my short

102

dance with her was more refreshing than most things out here. The Club is magnificent and demonstrates yet again the futility of the white man's grave theory. There were houses bordering the golf course as good as anything at Denham, and now in war they are living in perfect peace.

12 September 1941 – It opened with momentous news given most casually that America had declared war, later to be reduced merely to a 'shoot on sight' order to the Navy. But even that made me want to paint stars and stripes all over the ship so amazed was I at the apathy of everyone else. In the afternoon we had a great hockey match against the police on the local ground to which all the local enthusiasts turned out, cheering at the appropriate moments. It was an exceedingly sporting game and would have been equally enjoyable had it not been so tiring. I had to mark the best man in Lagos who was very much too fast for me. Afterwards the local photographer took our photographs with due ceremony. Of the two whites, one is most charming and impressive, more the Empire Builder type than I have seen – tall and thin with immense natural dignity, yet talking to the natives quite normally. He prefers the Bush to Lagos and complains strongly of having been brought here. His first job was on the frontier where he was entirely by himself for months on end; most of the rest of the time he has been on the small stations. Hence no doubt the cultivation of an aloof manner. In the evening a friend of the Captain's came to dinner with his wife, making the wardroom quite civilized, only disturbed by the accordionists and an Army sergeant who sang. Later we moved on deck where the singing was exceptionally good. Before dinner, half for conversation and half to drop a hint, I asked Coles what the chances were of getting inland and he (mildly amused I think) said he would try to arrange something for me. And now, this morning, he did. Apparently there is something very small going at the crack of dawn on the 16th and returning on the 17th, providing my own food and means of shelter of which there is none. It seems definite I shall go. I am most keen to do so and the Captain is willing. After all I haven't slept out of the ship for nine months – now I don't suppose I shall sleep!

I have been feeling desperately tired today and shall turn in really early to try to get over it. There is no peace though at this game unless it be just before I turn in. This cabin is a luxury certainly. Tomorrow we move into dry dock.

<u>14/15 September</u> 1941 – Typically sportingly, Cleeves agreed. The skipper of one of the tugs in the harbour has agreed to take me setting off at 0630 tomorrow. There is not much I can take with me except a sleeping bag and, I suppose, some food. It should be interesting.

**And so it turned out to be. I remember the whole occasion very vividly.**

At a quarter to six I set off. It was still dark and as the boy took me across in the canoe I was distinctly apprehensive as to whether I would manage to find the Eld-Bota wharf. I decided to take a taxi and make for the United Africa Company Office. Fortunately that was the place and I found the small tug waiting. After numerous delays, including collecting a lighter, we set off.

The trip down the lagoon and then up the creek was not remarkable in that I saw roughly what I expected – flat country with low banks, occasionally luxurious grass but usually thinly wooded. At a small village there was practically nothing, just a few poor shacks, the United Africa Company office and the wharf for lighters. They obviously didn't often see whites, treating me with totally different respect from the spoilt Lagos and Freetown natives. One even carried my umbrella over my head for me and they all stood and stared, obviously wondering what I had come for. I realized there was not much point in staying there so, having discovered that Jibuti was only seventeen miles and that there was a lorry purporting to be a bus going there, I decided to catch it and hope for the best. I sat beside the driver – a place of honour.

It was an amusing drive, if only because every ten minutes the driver stopped to put in more petrol from a can he had, explaining that only to put a little in at a time saved petrol. I did not like to disillusion him. The country inland was a revelation to me. The natives seemed surprised to see me and the road amazed me in its English appearance with grass banks and typical English ditches. But Jibuti seemed no better than the small village we had passed. I couldn't have spent the night there and there wasn't much to be seen, the natives still being so unspoilt that they don't trouble to make anything for an English market.

It was difficult to know where to get out. The European golf club, so called, was the only chance left and that was shut. But there was a notice saying it would open at 5.30 so I went for a stroll across the golf course and enviously looked at the enormous European houses

104

with their perfect views across lovely tropical gardens and the golf course to the wild bush. I prayed someone would invite me to stay the night and didn't look forward at all to returning. Someone did. I had been waiting in the club for a quarter of an hour or so when a man and his wife appeared and, on my excusing myself, sat down and talked. They were most charming and the husband even suggested I might like a game of golf with his wife. But it rained. Then I discovered that Morgan (the Inspector of Police from Lagos) was there. I had met him in Lagos. He expressed amazement at finding me there. He was most welcoming. From then on everything was perfect. It was arranged that I should spend the night with the District Officer and that my luggage should be collected from the river by taxi and that Cooper (another policeman) should take me back by road in the morning. I was relieved and happy. Morgan was most kind. He said I would never survive a night on the river. After a bath and change we went to the Bank Manager's house where a poker party was to take place. I had been warned by Morgan and backed out just in time. He explained that they would win or lose quite a lot which did not matter as it would cancel out as they played often. Also they paid a high percentage of their winnings to a Spitfire fund which they had started. There was a good dinner and I happily thought, the whole time, of a night in a comfortable bed. I thought of many other things too whilst they were playing but they were all vague and sentimental. We got back by 12.30 and sat for half an hour talking with Rex Gard. His, though, was a forced cheeriness and I could think only of the tragedy of his wife. It must be very lonely for him. I shall remember him – and Morgan – as a fine man doing a job which is not appreciated half enough. I went to sleep happier than for nine months (rather rudely disturbed by Cooper's bad manipulation of the petrol lamp) and woke even more so, quite overwhelmed by the lovely view from my bed across the golf course. Tea was brought to me and I got up very slowly. Before breakfast – which we didn't have till ten – Morgan said goodbye and Cooper showed me round the garden and the Resident's where I signed the book. Then we had to leave and I was very sorry. The drive back was fine, particularly the two hours in Abeocuta, having lunch with Layton, a fine character, and seeing the Alacci.*

* Head Man of one of the tribes in Nigeria.

The visit to the Alacci was intriguing. He had his daughter with him who was then twenty-two or so and had been at Oxford. To my great excitement and feeling of considerable anticipation he told her to go to his safe and gave her the key. I had a picture of a bar of gold at least. In due course she returned with a package which did not look much like a bar of gold. But as if it were, he took it from her and proceeded to open it when I confess to my disappointment I saw it to be a box of Cadbury's George V chocolates. With considerable ceremony he passed them to me. I realized they meant a good deal more to him than gold. I did my best not to look disappointed.

It was a holiday and I realized it even more as we drove into Lagos in the dark, feeling rather as I used to when arriving home from Minsmere.

**I was vividly reminded of the expedition when many years later I went to Lagos on the occasion of the Commonwealth Law Conference and, by extraordinary chance, met at dinner the Alacci's son (or it may have been his nephew). We were able to talk of those days long ago. I remember the occasion also when there was heavy rain during dinner which resulted in the outside area where we were dining being flooded at a depth of at least a foot when my wife pointed out to me that her long evening dress was awash but our hosts did not seem at all concerned. The strange occasion brought back many memories.**

19 September 1941 – It doesn't look as if I shall ever have a chance to write of all I have been doing lately. Tonight we have had a big sherry party on the boat deck to which we invited all the people we have met in Lagos. It was good and the setting better, with the accordionists and the sergeant singing. But afterwards there were complications with the girls we met last night at the Coles' dance – shall I have to rely on remembering it, or shall I have time to write of it? – of that and more general things – Colonial Service, Nigerian Police etc?

Hockey again against the police 1 – 1 but a poor game and scrappy.

**It was a strange life in Freetown, and equally so in Lagos and Takoradi. Superficially we seemed very much cut off from the war but we knew all too well of the dangers when we sailed. There were still unpleasant losses as a result of attacks from the German Armed Merchant Cruisers and those of their capital ships which were in the South Atlantic and**

106

continuing to cause much anxiety. But it was a very different life from the North Atlantic.

20 September 1941 – Our last day and not a very successful one for me as I couldn't get away from the Captain. And I felt the whole time as though I were making one last desperate clutch at luxury before sinking. I had wanted to sail, have dinner at the Grand and go to a flick – by myself – but instead I had to go out with the Captain. Even my call on Miss Campbell could not be done without him so that it was only after sandwiches and coffee when I at last went to the pictures by myself that I got to myself. Then I was sentimental, bought chocolates and lemon squash, but only fell asleep for at least half the film. When I got back the dance was in full swing and the Lagos elite were well shown off. That depressed me more still. I felt so insignificant and talk of glorious Navy so futile. It seemed no one cared; they had their dancing, their comfortable houses and unrationed food. It meant nothing to them; they couldn't afford to let it. Only the fat old French pilot who was shot down in Egypt knew – 'If I were going to sea tomorrow I would be drinking and dancing as much as I could, by God'. It is not that we have a hard time at sea – far from it – but there is something strangely lonely and frightening in leaving port and happy people preparing their Sunday evening dinner.

22 September 1941 – It is quite uneventful. We are only doing eleven so shall not be in until Friday morning – that is if we escape signals which would be a miracle. We are all tired and all probably praying there may be some news in Freetown. At least there will be letters. I must write some but it has suddenly become desperately difficult.

23 September 1941 – Have started a letter home at last but it is difficult I suppose because I haven't been able to write for so long and have too much to say. Energy is less than it was too; I still haven't finished writing of my drive back with Cooper. News that Romania is going to back out and Leningrad is still there. My God, if only they could do it. As I said to someone the other day, I'm sure I shall burst into tears when I get into an English train again.

26 September 1941 – At last the news that we have all always hoped for on getting back to Freetown has arrived. We got in just before breakfast, oiled, and were no sooner anchored than we had a signal

that we would probably be required for sea p.m. That was a blow but still it didn't really make any material difference. But then the Captain went across to *Edinburgh Castle* and came back with the momentous news that eight corvettes were to go home and that we were eighth on the list. It seemed perfect. We were due to go with the next convoy or one after next. But then we became suspicious and now we are considerably more so. Why did they choose to send us on this job? Can it all be a tragic 'frame up' to get us out of the port whilst someone else sails in our place. Aren't they, as the Captain insists, perhaps again going to lay a premium on efficiency? It is too tragic to think of and our one thought is to get back to Freetown as soon as possible. It is beginning to dawn on the Captain who swears blue murder, it is impossible to express the atmosphere of the ship. Everyone knows of it and tonight as we sailed past *Cyclamen* and *Columbine* and they shouted 'What about doing some sea time?', the others shouted back, 'We're going home'. That is all we can think of, though I have had some fine letters, long overdue. Are we really going home at last or are they going to do the dirty on us again?

27 September 1941 – Suspense has now become intense, so much so that the Captain cleared lower deck today and in moving terms explained the position, warning the men not to be too optimistic – which of course they are. He did it well, with considerable emotion, so that I gather they are now sorry for him and anxious he shouldn't take it too seriously. But they, poor fellows, will have something to say if it doesn't come off. It is so exasperating to be escorting this tanker knowing that all the time the others are probably organizing their homegoing.

> That is the land of lost content
> I see it shining, plain.
> The happy highways where I went
> And cannot come again.

Gwen can certainly write thoroughly good letters, quoting Housman here. I heard from Susanne at the same time, the first letter for two years now, in which she expresses similar feelings in a different way – 'Then I can only make the same date with you as a famous Czech soldier made with his friend; "I'll meet you at 4.30 after the war", but John be punctual'.

It is a dreadful feeling, this not knowing whether we are going home or not. We must all be the same: we must all have imagined by now exactly what our first sensations will be on arriving and must have planned how best to enjoy any leave we get. In our excitement we forget of course what we are returning to – another winter in the North Western Approaches, buffeting about round Iceland perhaps this Christmas – or maybe wandering round here still.

<u>29 September 1941</u> – Instead of less, we are now yet more on edge. I am reduced to a strange state of at one moment incredible and tragic indifference and the next one of perhaps indifferent tragedy. For I have thought so much about going home now – and have looked forward to it so very much – that I am terrified lest, when I do get home, I shall find that there will never be any true rest until the war is over and that there will merely be a prolonging of inevitable agony.

Housman again – 'The Sage to the Young Man'

> Well is thy war begun;
>> Endure, be strong and strive;
> But think not, O my son,
>> To save thy soul alive.

<u>1 October 1941</u> – In this morning after a mad rush back to get here before the others went out. We have done it too. The atmosphere was tense as we came in and as we passed *Asphodel* became even more so – particularly when the Captain shouted to *Asphodel*, 'How are we sitting' and got thumbs down in reply. Now we find that the four of them, *Calendula*, *Asphodel*, *Cyclamen* and *Columbine*, are due to go on Saturday and we are to sail with them but return. But the Captain appears to be doing his best; he went over to see Captain D this morning and, so he assures us, told him straight out that he thought the whole thing unjust. The result is uncertain. D thereupon said that in any case we must go with nine, but is going to see C-in-C about possibility of changing *Cyclamen*. In the meantime we are all more on tenterhooks than ever. I still feel we shall go but it will be bad luck on some of the malaria cases. This afternoon I am staying aboard, reading and sleeping. My cabin is in a state of complete chaos and will remain so until the position is easier. Every few hours I picture myself running to the nearest telephone box; surely it can't fall flat after all this anticipation.

<u>2 October</u> 1941 – Now it really does look as if I shall be able to run to a telephone box soon – the great miracle has happened and it seems we shall go instead of *Cyclamen* – after all these dreadful rumours and doubts it has come at last, thank God. Yet what have we got before us – returning to the North Western Approaches at the end of October, to bombing and U-boats in larger numbers than before. It is strange tonight to think of it, ghastly almost.

<u>4 October 1941</u> – There were disasters but now we are all right again. Tomorrow at 4.30 we sail for home. It will take nearly a month – pray it may be peaceful.

# CHAPTER VII

# Homeward bound

<u>5 October 1941</u> – <u>Sunday morning</u> – Convoy formed up and steering for home. Afraid all we can all think of is getting there safely, like poor old Bell going down to Sheerness for the last time. We've got thirty-five U-boats known of between here and there and an area of 'acute' danger East of 20W off the Spanish coast and Brest – up for the afternoon watch.

It does indeed look like being an exciting trip. Tonight I sat on the boat deck in a deck chair – absolutely calm, a full moon and warm. Soon it will be wild seas, cold and dark, but will there be a comfortable armchair at the end of it. We are all highly strung now.

<u>7 October 1941</u> – U-boat reported immediately in our track. *Velox* and *Wrestler* joined for the night and an air escort was provided but nothing happened, which is surprising seeing as we are only doing six and a half knots. God knows when we shall get home at this speed. There is trouble about fuelling at the Azores too, the Portuguese obviously objecting to Ponta Delgada being used as a base. To make matters worse the Captain has got a bee in his bonnet about it – that we should not do more than seventy-five revs in the day and will not be able to have any more baths. But they must be using an immense amount of water forward. The ship looks more like a barge on a working day on the Grand Union Canal, with all the blue suits hanging out on the boat deck and blankets and winter clothing out to air.

The hands do very little about the decks in the forenoons now but I don't worry. It seems pointless to point out and they will want all their energy later on, as we shall ours. As yet the Captain isn't bad but I can see he will become very difficult soon, particularly when we get into the aircraft area.

111

8 October 1941 – Mild excitement when *Brilliant* carried out a counter attack at 11.30 tonight when I was on watch. Fortunately I was sufficiently awake to realize what was happening, but by the time we got there it was all over. Otherwise all has been peaceful; we had been going intolerably slowly, at five and a half knots, but finally *Brilliant* sent *Cyclamen* and *Clover* off to Bathurst with the stragglers and now we are doing eight and a half. We took some mail for *Cyclamen* and bade her goodbye amidst a certain amount of cheering – a great pity she can't come too.

9 October 1941 – *Stork* and *Wellington* finally joined at 12.30, *Brilliant* having by that time gone off to look for them and got lost herself. Now we are settled down again till the Azores – *Wellington* and *Stork* ahead, *Asphodel* starboard, *Columbine* astern and ourselves port. It still seems a long way and John and I are both desperately impatient, equally worried lest something should happen before we get there. Captain is still reasonable, though gradually getting worse.

Panic soon after that – big M.V. suddenly appeared, moving fast down the beam of convoy, presumably catching Lecky asleep. Considerable confusion as she wouldn't answer 'What ship' and we couldn't get in touch with *Wellington*. It was obvious it must be something innocent yet I couldn't help thinking of something more sinister. The Captain, on the other hand, was sure it was Vichy and had actually told them to call up *Wellington* on the R.T. Fortunately she signalled her name just in time.

Panic started in middle when we broke into R.T., probably from O.S.7, telling of sinking of (apparently) a munitions ship. Now this morning we have had a whole series of signals, starting with *Londonderry*'s 'Submarine bearing two hundred and sixty degrees six miles', followed by hundreds of others between *Weston* and *Brilliant*. They haven't got it though. *Londonderry* dropped a Dan Buoy where it dived and *Brilliant* is chasing at twenty-seven knots. It must have been waiting for one or the other of us – thirty miles off. I'm afraid there are bound to be a good many now. Already there are three reported between Cape Verde and Canaries.

11 October 1941 – Have just had the route from *Wellington*, which was cheering. It is very direct and we reach rendezvous with local escort on 23rd, but it's damnably close inshore. Presumably they are

112

relying on the submarines being out west, but it will be risky for aircraft. Getting considerably cooler now so that we can sleep at night without sweating. Morning watch this morning was quite wild and the sun had that cold, distant, appearance that it has up north.

13 October 1941 – Weather and ship still miraculously fine, the days now being just like an English summer and the sun is quite different producing sunburn much more easily. I suppose the atmosphere is clearer. It must be for we saw the Canaries this afternoon eighty-three miles off – the north-western island, La Palma. It seems most rash to have gone so unnecessarily close. They would hardly see us I suppose but it increases their chances. At the moment alerted by report – 'Five or six submarines, assisted by aircraft'. Let us hope they won't drift westward after that and run into us. I'm afraid we are bound to get one or the other though, but I don't mind so long as nothing gets out of Brest. We are more and more excited at getting home and all have more worries about it. Ten days today we meet the Local Escort.

14 October 1941 – When small details are quite unimportant one is always, it seems, the most conscious of them. As this evening, for instance, nothing is really important or worth remark except that we are still afloat, about thirty-two North and still unattacked. But as we were moving astern for the sweep all sorts of ridiculous thoughts persisted in disturbing me from what might otherwise be a mental coma. Perhaps it was the wild sky, the first really wild – cold – one we have seen. Anyhow I thought of many things and when I came down to my cabin looked round at all the small things which still seem almost to be trying to form a link with past and future – the calendar, with its photograph of beech woods in autumn, the writing case I bought in Tangier, the photograph of Peter in his army uniform (which I see merely as a face I knew and loved so well two years ago but which I know so slightly now). It's all so unreal. The sea is getting rougher now, the squalls more frequent and colder.

15 October 1941 – Bad tonight.

17 October 1941 – We are in Ponta Delgada now, arriving daylight this morning. Action stations at five when Captain – who was taking Cripps' watch, finally decided that ship one hundred yards on our

113

quarter was not *Asphodel* but a destroyer, which turned out to be *Croome,* Hunt Class, and also oiling. Finally at seven we came in, had a bad hour doing so, but have now oiled, provisioned, exchanged innumerable courtesy calls with Portuguese destroyer and are at anchor waiting for *Asphodel* to fuel. It hasn't been a rest physically at all but nervously I think it probably has. We feel much nearer home and it has made an excellent break in the meantime. We shan't rejoin the convoy until morning of nineteenth and then only four days to local escort. Last convoy copped it very badly here – seven out of eleven, survivors being landed.

18 October 1941 – *Asphodel* managed to slow up oiling considerably – to the Captain's annoyance and worry, until 7.30 so that we were able to get ashore for half an hour. That was good and interesting but very hurried and necessarily something unreal about it all. It seemed even more detached than in December, yet the people are surprisingly aware of their precarious position and actually thought *Bismark* etc. were on their way there. At 7.30 *Asphodel* came out and we set course for SC89 again which we should catch tomorrow evening. Nothing has happened to it yet. All the U-boats must be concentrating to North-West. *Broadway,* one of the innumerable escorts of SC48, has been torpedoed and the Germans claim to have sunk two destroyers. They say too that we have announced loss of *Fleurs de Lys.* Still that's only the fourth. We should be in by 26th so that next few days will be a test. *Croome* said there were a lot between here and 50N (she sank one and sighted two more) but I think they are mostly Italians. But Captain is very nervy and at tea today even turned to me and said 'My daughter will just be going to bed now'.

19 October 1941 – We picked them up at noon today and were with them by four. Now signalled by aircraft that there is no local escort available so we have to take them on the way. If we are lucky it will be all right but if once we are sighted I'm afraid we shall have a bad time without a destroyer here to catch them on the surface. Tonight for the first time there is a cold dampness in the air and I felt glad to get down to the warmth of the wardroom again. It was very dark too. We are all cheerful and the Captain good tempered but each knows what the other is thinking. The clocks go to Greenwich Mean Time tonight so I have forty minutes' sleep.

<u>2030</u> – Getting dangerously close now. *Columbine* has dropped out to look after M.V. and our route has been altered to Eastward direct to 55N11W. Aircraft will be worse I fear and there are two U-boats reported directly ahead. To make matters worse *Wellington* used R.T. to get *Columbine*. Sweep on first port of entry – Captain drew Berwick-on-Tweed.

<u>21 October 1941</u> – A ship was torpedoed ahead of us early this morning, so we have altered to northward. Thought that we have been reported now too. Had a most unpleasant experience last night. There was a signal that L27 was routed twenty miles to eastward of us but we took precaution of warning *Asphodel* and were vaguely prepared to see her ourselves. I had just been wondering what I would do if I saw a U-boat on the surface that night when Lonegan – comparatively unconcerned – said 'What's this here?' It was a submarine only about three hundred yards off our port bow. At once I thought of L27 but was horrified lest it might not be her and there was so little time to make a decision. She identified herself and it was all over but it was a horrible moment as we swung round towards her. *Wellington* said this morning that she turned to ram and only just stopped in time.

<u>22 October 1941</u> – It started at four o'clock when we had 'Tally ho 0900 six miles' from *Wellington*, we having seen a submarine on the surface. We all went roaring off, *Stork* lumbering up from astern with whom we had a keen race much probably to his surprise (they managed 186 revs). Then the aircraft arrived, sighted it and attacked with bombs which we saw about four miles off. We swept the area as thoroughly as possible but found nothing so swept past the convoy and astern, *Asphodel* having by then dropped out of the chase. In the meantime signals had been flying about and C-in-C had altered route to 1800 Fastnet Rock ten miles which meant we were going round south in a desperate effort to evade the U-boats who must then have been coming in from all sides. *Beverley*, an American, was told to join. But it was no good. We were zigzagging furiously when at nine I saw a flash, explosion and ship go up. Thenceforth everyone did everything possible. We fired five of our starshells and the others fired more so that the whole horizon was incredibly well lit up. It was unpleasant and must have been much worse for the convoy. During the next hour or so *Wellington* reported a contact and then S.M. on the surface but

nothing more came of it. We charged about, avoiding *Beverley*'s starshell and going from one flare to another, during which time we certainly passed one boat which we got in the searchlight. Finally things began to quieten down, old *Columbine* piped up saying she had seen our gunfire and was doing her best to rejoin, and then we ran into *Asphodel*, picking up survivors, and so the story goes on.

2030 – The tension must have reached its climax now and is ghastly. In ten minutes this time last night a ship was torpedoed. Everyone is certain the same will happen again tonight and though I have been trying to convince myself that they have lost touch, I'm afraid I feel more like someone who knows he has to go to the dentist and longs to get it over. It is a cruel business. It was bad for Bell going down to Sheerness but this is much worse and more protracted. I shall turn in now and try to get to sleep. If I'm not woken before four, we should be all right, at least so far as U-boats go. We should be off the Fastnet tomorrow night and Liverpool by Saturday.

   Climax – a sudden signal to proceed North of Ireland – 'An attack on SL89 by enemy destroyers is possible tonight' – besides which *Prinz Eugen* is said to be nearing Brest for some purpose.

24 October 1941 – Presumably neither *Prinz Eugen* nor the destroyers did and now the outlook is much brighter. Tomorrow morning they split, by dusk *Wellington, Columbine* and ourselves will proceed Liverpool. So this is our last night with SL89 and I have it off – the first since some time before the Azores. We are all anxiously cheerful tonight. There are, according to submarine report fifteen between 51-54N but west of 20W so we should be all right. And danger from the air should be getting less. On the whole we have had a very good record. Altercation with *Stork* last night and this morning; claimed we were out of station during flap and this morning Captain sent 'With reference to your efficiency drive last night it was rather spoilt by having to ask for your course soon afterwards'. He sent two-page signal in reply, very hurt and annoyed.

   Should be due at 1800 tomorrow the Captain tells me. Thank God.

25 October 1941 – It was a beautiful morning with just a fine mist hanging round the horizon as the sun rose. The sea was almost flat, only disturbed by those ripples quite peculiar to an English autumn day. Now we can see land quite clearly and in an hour or so will leave

116

the remains of the convoy for good. They split at eight this morning, a sight which would surely have annoyed Hitler, nineteen fully loaded merchant ships and six escorts which he has chased the whole way from Freetown for three weeks, during which he only managed to get one and that possibly at the cost of a U-boat. But to me, regretfully most important of all, we are nearly back in England.

27 October 1941 – I suppose this is the time I have been waiting for for eleven months – sitting by myself in the wardroom by the light of an oil lamp again waiting for my turn to go on leave. But I feel there is something so desperately relentless about life. No one seems really to care what happens to us now. It might truly only be yesterday.

Extraordinarily news had leaked out of our parrot in the ship. We had the notice of which a copy follows. I am glad to say that it was not destroyed but sailed with *Clematis* again.

I was sad to leave *Clematis* and particularly Commander Cleeves. We had seen a great deal of action but one occasion I remember particularly well was in about September 1940 when Cleeves got us all together and said that he thought we should decide what to do if England were to fall to the Germans. He thought there were three alternatives. One was to surrender, another was to steam as far as we could across the Atlantic to America, depending on how much oil we had got, and the third option, which was typical of Cleeves, was to mount an invasion of Africa. We all voted in favour of steaming across the Atlantic. It demonstrates how critical things were in those days. Certainly losses were frightening. One of the worst occasions was a convoy with which we had sailed from Halifax, Nova Scotia, and in which thirty-seven out of fifty-two ships were lost in three nights. Commander Cleeves was on the bridge for three days and nights without sleep and remained calm throughout in spite of everything, including intensive rescue work. I find it difficult sixty years later to remember the horror of it all.

Of course, the person upon whom by far the greatest responsibility lay in any ship was the Captain. Cleeves was one of the finest examples of a fine seaman and a great leader. We were very sorry indeed when he left *Clematis* to be relieved by another officer. He had not only had an exceptionally fine record during the war, but also when it was over was very kind to me when faced with the problem of finding a job. Soon after I had qualified as a solicitor, he recommended me to an appointment as Secretary of the Pilots Association, from which a well known member of the Bar, Inskip, was retiring. But I was not appointed. At that stage I

[7095] 44721/8973 30 pads 3/39 2076 G & S 704

# MINISTRY OF HEALTH.

PORT OF *Liverpool*

To *The Master*

*S.S. C. Clematis*

In pursuance of the Parrots (Prohibition of Import) Regulations, 1930,
I hereby give you notice that the parrot(s) (1) on board
~~being landed from the~~
(2) *S.S. C. Clematis* shall not be removed from
(3) *S.S. C. Clematis* for any purpose other than exportation.
Unless a written undertaking that you will within three days, or such
longer period as the ship may remain in the port, export the parrot(s) at
your own expense is received by me by (4) *Oct 31st/41*
..................the parrot(s) will be destroyed.

Signature *[signature]*

Medical Officer of Health.

Date *27 . 10 . 41*

(1) *Strike out words not required.*
(2) *Insert name of ship.*
(3) *Insert name of ship or other appointed place.*
(4) *Insert date and time.*

NOTE.—The Public Health Act, 1896, provides by sub-section (3) of section 1 that if any person
wilfully neglects or refuses to obey or carry out, or obstructs the execution of any regulation
made under any of the enactments mentioned in that Act, he shall be liable to a penalty not
exceeding £100, and, in the case of a continuing offence, to a further penalty not exceeding £50
for every day during which the offence continues.

Port 15.

certainly had not got the qualifications required. When he died, I was particularly sorry to be unable to go to his memorial service in 1965 but I have got a copy of the memorial address, which follows. I would like at this stage to add my unlimited admiration for the man he was. Throughout his days in the Navy he demonstrated great courage and skill. That was no less true of his time in *Clematis*. After the North Atlantic, life in the South Atlantic may seem to have been less dangerous. In fact *Clematis* was a valuable addition to the other escorts in that area. The danger of U-boats, capital ships and armed merchant cruisers was very much greater than appeared on the surface. The fact is that *Clematis*, and indeed Cleeves, had a charmed life.

The Memorial Address given at St. Mary's Church, Swansea, on Wednesday, 2 June 1965 in honour of Captain Yorke McLeod Cleeves DSC, DSO, RD, RNR reflected the remarkable man he was.

Captain Yorke McLeod Cleeves DSC, DSO, RD, RNR served his King and Country in the two World Wars with great distinction. A son of Gower, he retained his love of Gower to the end and returned to spend there the last years of his retirement. To his early days on Gower with its beautiful coastline he owed his love of ships and the sea.

Captain Yorke Cleeves joined the RNR in 1925. He kept in touch with all the latest developments, and at the outset of the Second World War was immediately called to serve

He was placed in charge of minesweeping operations in Northern Waters and received his DSC for 'unfailing courage, endurance, resource, and devotion to duty in the hard and perilous task of sweeping the seas clear of mine combatting submarines, and keeping a look-out for the enemy'. So reads the official citation. In May 1940 Captain Cleeves was on board and in command of the *Warwickshire* with five of His Majesty's Trawlers in the Trondheim area when all were sunk through Nazi air bombing attacks.

In August of the same year he was awarded the DSO for 'courage, initiative and devotion to duty on service in His Majesty's Trawlers in the Romsdal Fjords'.

Later in the war he was on duty in the North and South Atlantic. Whilst Senior Officer on escort duty aboard the *Clematis* in the North Atlantic thirty-seven out of fifty-two ships in the convoy were lost in two nights. One who was there has said of him that he was on the bridge for three days and nights without sleep, and that throughout the whole period he remained cool and calm amidst all

119

the turmoil and noise of battle, the clamour of activity and rescue work.

Captain Yorke Cleeves was an officer of the highest calibre, a qualified Navigation Officer, a qualified Minesweeping Officer, a qualified anti-Submarine Officer and a man of sterling character. Swansea and the Gower may be justly proud of him.

After Commander Cleeves had left us, we continued with the North Atlantic convoys with a different Captain. He was an RNVR Lieutenant Commander, which was quite unusual at that stage in the war. There were again the usual dangers and excitements. Although once or twice we thought we had sunk a U-boat, it was never easy to be sure unless significant wreckage reached the surface.

As I have said elsewhere, it is difficult now to accept that one was pleased to sink a U-boat and had no feelings for those who had been drowned in it. But no doubt it is inevitable that wars will always distort the characters of those involved in them. It is only the very small minority of populations who share responsibility for the consequences of their decisions. But there are also the occasional happy consequences for those who are fortunate enough to have the opportunity to take advantage of them. Certainly that was so in my case.

We went into Plymouth for a boiler clean when John Ellyatt's sister was a boating Wren there. I had met her on Paddington Station as a schoolgirl from Sherborne. It was too good a chance to miss. I asked John Ellyatt if I might take his sister out for the evening. 'I wish you would,' he said, and so it started.

# CHAPTER VIII

# HMS *Exe* in North Africa
# and the Battle of the Atlantic

It was indeed very sad to leave *Clematis* but one tended to be appointed to another ship after two years. I was appointed to *Exe*. She was one of the River class frigates and appreciably larger than *Clematis*. Again she was primarily for anti-submarine work but was also a minesweeper. The first captain, Commander Freaker, was another fine seaman who among other things had a Polar Medal. I still remember well our first night at Tobermory under the eye of the great Admiral Stephenson. It was a particularly good September evening. In a stupid moment I said to Freaker how good it would be to have a swim before breakfast next morning. He immediately agreed and said 'Let us meet on the foredeck at seven o'clock'. We did meet but only briefly in that he immediately dived in, which was the last thing I intended to do, and felt distinctly inferior when I walked down the gangway and simply stepped in. Clearly Freaker did not get his Polar Medal for nothing. *Exe* was the first of the escorts to have what was then the new anti-submarine armament of hedgehogs, which were very different from the depth charges one had previously. Instead of dropping depth charges over the stern you fired something equivalent over the bows. I remember it all well because it was my responsibility. The Battle of the Atlantic was then at its peak and we were very fully employed. The losses were fearful but we survived. A sad example of those days was the fate of the First Lieutenant of *Clematis*. After he left us I had been appointed First Lieutenant by Cleeves. I am not sure which his ship then was but I was told that during one particularly bad night they were sunk. He was picked up only to be sunk again and lost. His name appears among all those thousands of others on the memorial on Plymouth Hoe.

I had been appointed as the Anti-Submarine Officer in *Exe*. As I have said, she was one of the first, if not the first, to have hedgehogs, so that, whereas previously one had got used to dropping depth charges astern as you went over the position as you hoped of the U-boat, you now picked the U-boat up on AS as it was called, recorded the distance ahead as it closed and then, at the appropriate moment, fired the hedgehogs. It was proved to have been a more effective way of dealing with U-boats and became fitted in more and more of the escort ships. We were involved in *Exe* in a number of anti-U-boat actions but were never able to prove that we had sunk any of them. However, life was still distinctly hazardous.

We were suprised, I think it is true to say, after the North Atlantic, to have had instructions to join what became known as Operation Torch. I think that perhaps the reason was that we were also a minesweeper and had in command Commander Biddulph, who had had a lot of experience of minesweeping. Fortunately we never had to do it. I remember the exercise which I fear made it pretty clear that we would have been in danger of making a mess of it.

Commander Biddulph was yet another remarkable character. I cannot really remember why it was but he was known to us officers as 'father'. Certainly no one could have been more considerate, efficient or kinder. Perhaps that was why. I remember that when on the bridge he chose to sit, which was unusual, facing aft. He explained that we all kept a lookout forward but that it was important that someone should look aft.

Much of my diary then deals with the preliminaries of Operation Torch and the operation itself after the enormous convoy had got to North Africa via Gibraltar. One realizes now that the risks were enormous as the evidence of our own losses demonstrate. But losses could have been very much worse. One problem which had to be dealt with was that part of the French Fleet still in North Africa. During the succeeding months there were many incidents. The worst perhaps concerned the British ships *Walney* and *Hartland*, which purported to be American in the hope that when entering Oran the French would accept them, since they were not flying white ensigns. I have referred to them again later.

My diary follows:-

Tuesday, 29 July 1943 – The last time I wrote anything in my diary was 20 July when we commissioned. I still have it but think it will probably be wiser to keep this small notebook rather than a large diary now. For it seems much is going to happen in a fortnight's time. We left Gourock pier at 6.30 this morning for the oiler and after swinging for compasses, collecting a last mail in our motor boat, sailed 'in execution of previous orders'. It was a lovely autumn day, almost a flat calm, with that dim watery sun. The 'tail of the bank' was strangely quiet and deserted compared with the last few weeks. The 'Spanish Armada' had sailed. Tomorrow at 6 am we are due to join them. Where we are bound we still don't know, other than that it is approximately a fourteen day passage. I do know we are going towards Gib. We shall be there presumably in about eight days. From there still six days to go. That would just take us either to Benghazi or Dakar. Which will it be? Are we going close to Gib to give the impression it is a Malta convoy and then turning South, or are we going straight through and has all the Dakar publicity lately been intentional? I know we all long for the next fourteen days to go quickly. Yet it must be far worse for the Commandos in the troop-ships. It is still calm just rolling slightly now. Tonight I have the first watch.

<u>Wednesday – 10 August</u> – Rumours are slowly piling up, father finding it desperately difficult to keep things to himself. It now seems we shan't start back until after Christmas – also wherever it is is tideless – the Mediterranean surely? Yet I still can't see how they are going to get this enormous convey in, as well as the many others there seem to be, and the aircraft carriers and battlewagons. We are doing a steady 11½. Pray the submarines don't find this enormous target. Peter's birthday today. This time last year I had just gone on leave.

<u>Thursday, – 31</u> – Nothing much today except that on reading the *Weekly Times* I see Hitler in his latest speech talked of us as a nation as 'militarily imbecile' and, referring to the second front, capable 'of any mad enterprise'. I hope he isn't right. It does seem we take the most fearful risks: it is ghastly to think of the possibility of one of this convoy being torpedoed with its cargo of some 4,000 troops. However all goes well so far. We had a doubtful contact this afternoon and dropped one charge amidst considerable excitement, poor old father quite unable to think of anything but minesweeping. The weather has been excellent, warm enough this afternoon to sit on deck, although we are still 49N.

<u>Friday</u> – Weather still good, although deteriorating a little now. Tomorrow we should oil – *Roth*er and *Swale* have done so today from *Sheffield* but it's only fifty tons an hour so a slow process. *Biter* flew off AC today for the first time. Otherwise nothing, still speculation. Theory is now Oran and Algiers and getting Rommel in the rear via

123

Tunisia. But in that case why can't we oil at Gib? The convoy exercises anti-aircraft armament every forenoon – a fearsome barrage.

<u>Sunday</u> – am – Another perfect day – yesterday not so good so that we couldn't oil as planned. Doing so today from *Sheffield*. At the moment we are screening whilst *Rother* oils and then vice versa. We are about 42 N now. The convoy is an encouraging sight from here: even out of my scuttle I can see *Sheffield* in the foreground with this enormous convoy beyond. It would disconcert the Germans. Surely no country that is in any danger of losing the war could send a convoy like this into the Atlantic – and with only one cruiser. It would cheer the people at home and perhaps even Aneurin Bevan would keep quiet about the second front.

<u>pm</u> – *Sheffield* has had to give up oiling, *Rother* having broken the springs, was told to do it instead, using the floating hose method. After a few preliminary difficulties this was successful. By 1730 we had taken in 190 tons. It was a strangely stirring sight when we left her, for we steamed past very close playing 'Anchors Aweigh' and 'Hoist the jib and spanker' on the loud hailer whilst thousands of mostly American troops gathered on deck. We had been playing it during the afternoon and many of them had collected on the poop but there was something very stirring about this.

A marine died aboard one of the other ships and colours were half-masted from 4.30 – 5.30. As the Captain said, 'He little dreamed he would be buried in mid-Atlantic when he left home.' Meanwhile *Biter*'s AC reported a U-boat astern; apparently there are many round us. We go through the straits in the dark in about 2 days, then. Sicily is the latest..

<u>Monday</u> – A day of disaster in most ways. Were going to transfer confidential books from *Clare* this evening but AC was seen to drop bomb and use tracer. Rushed towards it, searched frantically, and then had a signal that it was only jettisoning depth charges. Then continued with transferring operation in the middle of which QM went Port 20 instead of Port 2 the result being we crashed into *Clare* (a truly sickening and horrible moment) – parted the line plus books, not to mention causing her steering gear to jam. We had the end of the grass on the bridge but couldn't hold it and it finally took the wing bridge dodger with it, splintering violently but fortunately triplex,

124

otherwise my hand would have suffered. Thus horrible visions of all secret books of the operation floating about on the surface, for when we hauled in the stray end we found grass had parted. However miraculously bag had been weighted by *Clare*. Considerable confusion ensued. Now we are rejoining convoy with Radio Direction Finding broken down expecting to hit it any moment. However, father has lightened situation by telling us all the plans. They seem excellent and, on paper certainly, should go easily. But will they? If they do, if Russia holds out until winter and then drives Germans back, war should be over by next winter. It is cheering.

Thursday – (D-3) – Yesterday the convoy split, *Jamaica*, and the destroyers joining the Algiers portion, proceeding so as to get eleven hours ahead of us. There is still no sign of an attack on the convoy, strangely as there are nine U-boats making toward Gib – which suggests they are beginning to smell a rat. But there isn't much they can do about it now. At the same time the Eighth Army is driving Rommel before them. When he hears we have landed and are marching to take him in the rear in Tunisia he will be in a very unpleasant position.

Friday evening 7 – Almost the eve of the battle now, no one knowing what is likely to happen. I have just been out on deck to see the lights of Tangier on our starboard beam. It is strange – this huge troop convoy slipping through the straights at night and difficult to realize its significance. This time tomorrow night we should be nearly sighting the lights of Oran. At 0100 the assault craft and destroyers go close in. At 0530 we go right in with the rest and then do an A/S patrol a mile offshore. Anything might happen. At the moment we are SO of the escort while *Westcott* goes into Gib for fuel. At least the weather is fine, though the wind is freshening now.

Saturday – 2050 – Just going up to Action Stations now until the morning. Situation certainly tense.

Sunday – In now and the landing well advanced. It all went fairly well according to plan except the confusion in our section when we were due to leave the Malta section. However, it went off all right and we arrived at 0530. Then, almost light, a few mysterious and frightening things were happening. There was still considerable firing ashore with occasional tracer flying about and very heavy stuff to the N'ward, apparently afterwards found to be *Aurora* finding a French destroyer and *Rodney* bombarding a shore battery – which we could see. At that time too a signal came through saying that all landings had been successful except at B beach, but that fighting was still going on at Arzeu and programme was thus a little behind. However, now all is extraordinarily quiet in spite of Petain's appeal to the French to fight – they hadn't much chance.

The only things that can cause trouble now are the French fleet from Toulon, the Italian fleet or aircraft. According to situation reports, the French have not moved nor the Italians from Taranto. Aircraft have a long way to come. There is still time, though, for plenty. How long we shall stay is still not certain. It rather depends on whether the minesweepers arrive or whether we shall have the job of sweeping into Oran. Meanwhile we all wonder how *Hartland* and *Walney* are getting on in Oran. They must have had a distinctly hot time.

Monday – We are alongside an oiler now with *Brilliant* outside us. The position seems to be that Arzeu beach is in our hands all right and Algiers has surrendered but Oran is still fighting and the French Navy being troublesome. So far two French destroyers have been sunk, one by *Brilliant* and one by *Aurora*, and just now a battle is going on off here, two more having got mixed up with *Furious* and started firing torpedoes. They can't have much chance. They must have been trying to creep out of Oran for they were picked up first close inshore near our endless chain patrol. *Rodney* and *Aurora* started bombarding this morning too but fired very little so perhaps it is now nearly over. So far, as far as we know, *Hartland, Walney* and *Gardenia* have been sunk. Losses amongst American troops have not been announced at all. The whole position is thus still confused and uncertain – how much longer we shall be here etc. Presumably we shall have to go on doing this endless chain for some time. And will the Toulon fleet come out? I should think there is every chance of it. Apparently, though, Vichy losses off Casablanca have been very heavy already so maybe they will be discouraged. At the same time rumour has it that we are to be based here.

A perfect day today – everyone in whites – and difficult to realize all this is going on ashore and battles at sea which we may get mixed up in any moment.

126

Tuesday – We have lost two more destroyers – *Broke* and another – although it is not yet known how. Oran still just holds out although there is now news that tanks have been landed. For us news is no better than in England. We can hear the firing going on and get the signals asking for dive bombers to bomb a certain target but otherwise do little more than patrol off this bay full of ships. The French must have had enough of it, yet one feels they deserve all they get after the sinking of *Walney* and *Hartland*. A demand this morning for *Albatross* to bomb the nine-inch battery at Cape Canastel but they have been told to stop now. That is going on everywhere.

Disaster in the chain patrol the other night, *Felixstowe* running down *Clacton* and nearly sinking both of them. It is not surprising wandering up and down there in the dark, half the ships without RDF, and no navigational lights ashore. We still wonder what will happen to us. It looks even more as if we might have to stay now that these other ships are out of it.

Thursday – All has changed. Since then Oran has capitulated and Germany has marched through unoccupied France. Cessation of hostilities in N. Africa has been ordered accordingly. At the same time Germans have landed parachutists in Tunisia as we and the Americans march towards it. A race has developed. News is very good, having clearly got Hitler rattled now. He has an enormous front to cover. A lot may depend on whether we get French fleet or not. At 1600 this evening we sail for Gib, presumably the first stage of return journey with first convoy and then out again with another. But so much seems liable to happen: news could hardly be better. We nearly went into Oran this afternoon but Gib instead. A good many ships being torpedoed including *Viceroy of India*.

Sunday – An uneventful trip to Gib, twenty-four hours in, and now out again with a small 13½ knots convoy home. Left yesterday evening with *Avenger* and seven MVs – plus *Amazon*, *Swale*, *Gloisdale*, *Wrestler* – *Argus* catching up later. At 0320 tracer was seen from *Wrestler* and DCs heard. Shortly afterwards attack developed. Now find that *Avenger* and *Altmark* torpedoed. We thought there was only one – terrific explosion and bits everywhere. It looked like an MV but must have been one silhouetted against the explosion. Now *Wrestler* is rejoining after searching amongst oil (apparently nothing else) and *Gloisdale* is standing by *Altmark* who is still afloat

127

but sinking; they have abandoned ship. This positon is rather gloomy, still having a long way to go through bad waters and close inshore. Of course it's always the same coming out of Gib: there were known to be mines in the approaches. But if we get through tonight it should be all right and it's difficult to believe a U-boat could shadow at this speed – a good 13½!

Sunday night – Everything very tense now. Discovered that three ships were torpedoed last night – must have totalled good 50,000 tons. Now we are surrounded with U-boats again and have only four escorts. With any luck we may get through. Have managed a Heath Robinson repair on our A/S – tied up with string and asbestos (good work by Dan). Made a diagram for the RDF too. It seems to work strangely. Now appears that echo was reported last night by RDF Red 5 13,000 but not acted on by Younger. Let's hope for best.

Shall have a good sleep anyhow.

Monday – Only one alarm at 2320 when *Amazon* and *Wrestler* both had echo by RDF but if it was sub it was put down for nothing more happened. Yesterday I just heard the last of the Church bells to celebrate the Egyptian victory. England is all jubilation. I pray it is not too soon. So much may still go wrong. And are they right, I wonder, to rejoice whilst people are still being killed? *Avenger* – she steamed past us on Saturday, piping in Gib harbour with many standing up on the decks full of life – was blown up that night. If they had seen that, if they had seen perhaps one of our victorious Egyptian planes crashing in flames, would they still have felt like ringing the Church bells the next day? Tonight we should be all right for, according to situation reports, we are out of the area now, the thickest of it. Route was altered further to eastward and looks as if we shall go south about.

Heard incidentally from the Captain that there were seventeen on the bridge of *Hartland* of whom sixteen were killed, many more being shot at in the water. The only survivor was Captain Peters and he was killed when AC he was going home in crashed. Most of that news came from Lieutenant Commander Woodruffe of BBC fame who was aboard here with father in Gib, having drunk more than was good for him. In that state it appears he told far more than he should have done but according to Captain it is all cheering – except that initial losses in Arzeu landing were heavy.

The news of *Walney* and *Hartland*, who had sailed out to North Africa with us, was indeed very sad.

<u>Friday</u> – All went smoothly after that and, zigzagging furiously all the way, we are now nearly there – minus *Amazon* and *Wrestler* who ran out of fuel and had to make a dash for Moville. *Argus* has rather done the dirty on us, making us continue nearly to Kintyre before leaving which is going to mean we shan't get to oiler until one in the morning, leaving thus only a small margin for getting up river in time for the 2.45. That is if there is leave. It can't be much for, by our calculations, we are due to leave with KMF4 again at the end of the week.

<u>28 November – Saturday</u> – We didn't get any leave, Commander Unwin's BBC prediction having been only too true. We sailed from Derry on Thursday, spent Friday in the Clyde waiting for the convoy and are now with the same old lot all over again – *Orbita, Reno de Pacifico, Samuel Chase.* It is magnificient that they should have managed to turn round so quickly loading up with troops. Again it is a fast one and we are due to pass through the Straits on the night of the 5th. This time we should stop there but many rumours have it that we shall go straight on. As the Captain said, 'I hope not'. We have 150 bags of mail aboard and three RAF Sergeants – presumably for Gib. There has been little more news of N. Africa except that *Ibis* and *Tynwald* were lost too. Our escort this time is good – *Egret, Quickmatch, Tanatside, Banff, Clare, Swale* and selves. Weather is reasonable but even just the cold and dark begins to seem bad when it is so long since we have seen the lights of cities – or so it seems.

<u>Monday</u> – *Clare* left Saturday morning with boiler trouble but Admiralty unable to provide relief, so that convoy of twenty-six is escorted by only seven. Nothing yet except attacks on probably non-subs. One by us today. Possibly something this evening when soon after we had picked up RDF echo *Tanatside* and *Quickmatch* got the same and went to investigate. Apparently it had dived by the time they got there. So something may happen any moment. Otherwise orders from *Egret* to conserve DC's in view of heavy concentration of subs round approaches to Gib. Nine within 150 miles of us even here. How suddenly one's peace of mind can be disturbed. Was just thinking of going to sleep when alarms went. RDF echo. Slowly closed it. Ranges coming down then – 'Stand by to open fire' – 030 deflection four left.

Then realized to be two ships – one large one small – finally identified as straggler from MK54 and HMS *Dunbar*. Feelings a mixture of relief and disappointment – mostly relief.

Tuesday – A few more contacts and RDF echoes during the night but nothing developed. Now they have re-routed us again and a signal too to say we are bound for Algiers. Another one that a German Raider has sailed from Biscay port and may be intercepted by us. It would have a hot time with *Quickmatch*, *Tanatside* and *Egret* after it, I imagine. Not so good if we were only corvettes.

1700 – She ran straight into us. Sighted at 1427 by *Egret* she was closed by *Quickmatch* and *Tanatside*. What action took place is unknown but last signal was from *Egret* to *Quickmatch* 'Sink raider immediately and return to convoy'. Weather is very bad now so there can't be many survivors. Trouble is that they have reported our position. Latest news that it was Italian – explains their putting up little fight.

2300 – Getting very rough in patches now. *Quickmatch*, *Redoubt* and *Egret* have rejoined. Tomorrow *Farndale* and *Avondale* join from Gib. News this evening that *Manxman* has been torpedoed off Oran. Convoy had to reduce speed to eleven because *Banff* and *Tanatside* were finding the going too heavy. Due to pass straights 2200/4 now. This weather may hold us up badly if it lasts.

Thursday – 3 – Detached to go back to *City of Edinburgh* who has been having a bad time with her forward gun washed away and forepeak full of water, contracted during the heavy weather. If all goes well we may find her in the morning. Meanwhile KMF4 is miles away, so presumably we shall go into Gib and wait until *Egret* comes back unless they send us on of course. Woodruffe apparently spoke about Oran on the news tonight. They announced our N. African losses too – which we know *Walney*, *Hartland*, *Broke*, *Martin*, *Gardenia*, *Ibis*, *Avenger*, *Tynwald*.

Monday 7 – Everything went wrong. We couldn't find *City of Edinburgh* and then had a signal that she had arrived in Gib. We were told to proceed Gib at best speed but were then told to look for boatful of survivors in a position off Trafalgar which we have been doing ever since, now at last going in, arriving in the early morning.

In the midst of it we had a classic signal from FOCNA RAF launch or AC out of petrol. We did find it after firing about twenty starshells during the middle, switching on searchlights and generally attracting all the U-boats in the area. We started to take it in tow but the tow broke so we decided to leave it and search for survivors. All we found were two bodies, which was sickly, as they had obviously been in the water for a long time. It seemed possible they might have come from *Avenger*. It would do some people at home good to have seen it. Meanwhile *Tay* and *Wear* are sailing for home again tomorrow with a slow convoy. Presumably that means there will be a fast one for us very soon.

Tuesday – Arrived Gib yesterday at seven and after going to appointed oiler which had no oil had to stay on board until supposed meningitis was diagnosed as something else. By that time most were too tired to go ashore. At 3.30 am orders came to raise steam, and then later to sail at best speed to Oran to pick up KMS 4(Y). Thus we shall be very lucky to get home for Christmas at best seeming only likely to make the 24th. Indeed it may well be very wretched for one of those slow convoys is just about due for a party. We reach Oran at midnight, fuel and sail again at eight. At least, however, we shall have the boiler hours by Derry. Assuming we get back on the 24th it will be fifty-one days out of fifty-eight. *Stork* and *Marne* both in Gib torpedoed – *Stork* with her bows blown off, during endless chain of Algiers and *Marne* her stern, hit by torpedo fired at *Hecla*. It hit her in the magazine, so that you can see the shells exposed by the gaping wound. Incredible that they both got in. Nor were there very many casualties.

Wednesday – Finally arrived Oran at 1230 after difficulty in finding it due to lack of lights only to be told to proceed with all despatch to assistance of *Porcupine* torpedoed forty miles to westward. Finally found her in company with *Vanoc* at dawn, torpedoed in the engine room and with a 20 list. Took her in tow in quick time of seventeen minutes and are now proceeding Oran at five knots. Tug and two trawlers came out to meet us but it was decided that as we were doing so well we should carry on. She is a sorry sight – such a fine looking ship too. *Vanoc* took survivors all except captain, four officers and forty crew and took her in tow for a while until getting A/S contact when she slipped and we took over. Apparently there were only seven

131

casualties, presumably all engine room. It will be good to get her in, but it is sad to see her trailing along on our quarter so badly smashed up.

Thursday – Got her in, amidst many congratulatory signals, to Arzeu where we spent the night ourselves with *Vanoc* (until 11.30) although we felt we should go to Oran. Decided to go round at first light. When we came out ran straight into *Egret* with KMF4 which we had thought to be further ahead. Indeed we had been afraid we would miss them. It was immediately assumed that we were joining (our only orders of course were to join the mysterious KMS 4 (Y)). At 2 we were detached with *Bulalo*, Rear Admiral Burroughs and *Tanatside* to Gib, we to fuel and she to collect prisoners amongst other things. Now, at five, reported that *Blean the Hunt* who was immediately astern of us, and probably moved into our position, has been torpedoed and sunk – yet another example of luck being on our side. Apparently *Wishart* sighted periscope shortly before. It was most unfortunate, being whilst convoy was steaming back. Thus there is a flap again, and there would seem to be cause for it, a disastrous number of HM ships having been torpedoed, and *Bulalo* is fussing madly about the screen she is getting from us too. We arrive Gib at two and go in to fuel, *Tanatside* returning to the convoy. In the meantime *Sennen*, *Rother* and *Spey* have arrived Gib, *Sennen* to escort MRF 4, *Rother* and *Spey* unspecified. All may thus be well. What are *Rother* and *Spey* intended for? And do we sail again with *Bulalo* and MRF 4 or not?

Saturday – Arrived all right, anchored and finally got alongside oiler at five with orders to leave again at seven which were cancelled and amended to 9.30. *Tanatside* went at seven and we at 9.30 with *Bulalo* to join convoy outside. Now 9.30 pm approaching the zero hour for an attack. Passed the slow section in the straits, as well as a number of Carley Floats and lifebelts – certainly rather a graveyard.

Monday – Nothing developed, but last night very bad weather. During the middle there was a squall for quarter of an hour stronger than anything I have known. The whaler broke adrift and the RDF broke down, and then in the morning the griping spar of the MB went too. However the convoy was still there at dawn. *Egret* made a signal 'How are escorts getting on'. Reply from *Banff* was 'Have hung up my stockings' and *Sennen* 'Wet but not worried'. *Tanatside* wanted to reduce a knot. At least though it means U-boats are not likely to attack. Strange signal from S.O. Force 6 'Am being attacked by enemy A.C. 030 Cape Trafalgar 30 miles', followed five minutes later by '*Argonaut* torpedoed'. It seems a very strange position for enemy aircraft to be and looks rather as if they have started looking for convoys again.

Tuesday – Strangest of coincidences today. At 1230 sighted innocent-looking tanker on the horizon apparently hove to in the gale. By 1343 were close up to it when finally *Egret* detached *Tanatside* to investigate it. Just as *Tanatside* was closing her she blew up and (presumably) crew abandoned ship. Then discovered that she was German *Germania*. *Tanatside* put two torpedoes and gunfire into her but still she didn't sink. Crew, nine officers and sixty-two, were picked up and T rejoined by 1800. It was all over, quickly and mysteriously, and a 10,000-ton tanker is now probably on the bottom. One each way is extraordinarily good going, especially *Germania* who has been at large for so long. Where was she bound? It seemed she was light.

Weather is still very bad but most luckily astern of us. *Test* and *Fishguard* couldn't make it and are both hove to in 50 N. Seems we should now be in by Friday pm but latest buzz that we shall sail 26th again with KMF 61.

Wednesday – Moderating now a little. Convoys coming the other way are having a very bad time, hove to and scattered. Should be in a.m. Friday now which is better and better.

We finally got in earlier than anticipated, secured alongside the oiler by 2.30. But, after all the preparations for the White Christmas at home, got up river to find there was no leave and that we were to sail again with KMF 6 on Christmas Day.

Boxing Day – Sailed from Derry at three yesterday afternoon and had a great send off from all the children's party in *Tay* who gave a cheer as we passed. After considerable messing about, complicated by drunkenness of oilers' crew, we got alongside one and there spent the night merrymaking, sailing at 7.15 into a rolling head sea. Nevertheless I believe the weather is good. Swell caused large jug of milk to upset straight into my lap.

133

As well as a number of passengers and a whole lot of mail we took Alan Moorhead with us. He was, of course, a most excellent and interesting passenger to have. I remember after the war greatly enjoying his two books *The Blue Nile* and *The White Nile*. I am afraid my diary later tells of how badly treated he was by us when transferring him to another ship.

Monday 28 – Weather got worse later as we got clear of the land and wind freshened but it has cleared up again now and we have the inevitable following sea. No excitements – although tonight signal to say that several U-boats will be in our vicinity on passage. Weather is unusually warm.

Wednesday – We seem doomed. Signal from C-in-C hot today '*Exe* to be detached to arrive Londonderry January 4'. Complete disregard apparently for all the thirty-two passengers, bags of mail and Alan Moorhead. *Egret* made a signal 'Detaching *Exe* 0600 to Derry in accordance with your 1115. She has on board thirty-two passengers, fifty bags of mail and stores for Algiers.' However, we took compassion on Moorhead who was transferred to *Loyal*, resulting almost in an appalling disaster. When the order 'Stand by falls' was given they contrived to let go of the after fall altogether. It was a miracle they didn't all finish in the drink. Moorhead was remarkably calm. Hardy was left dangling on a lifeline. As bad was the getting aboard *Loyal* in the heavy swell. I don't suppose Moorhead will ever want to transfer at sea again. What we are in for is a complete mystery but it looks bad – perhaps oiling at Moville and then straight out again. Or are we wanted for something else?

No excitement at all as yet except night before last when *Loyal* thought she had something and fired numerous depth charges and starshell. Nothing. We have had echoes good and bad but only fired one depth charge and nothing there I think. Weather is moderate but it looks as if we may have a nasty plug into a head sea all the way home.

Sunday – Inevitably things have not gone according to plan. We were told to continue with the convoy, being detached when situation warranted. Finally we went on Friday morning due to arrive Gib 2200 but then had all the flap of transferring stores and personnel to *Nelson*, then going for oil. Expected to be off again in the morning but Gibraltar had got hold of us and didn't intend letting us go single-handed. Sailed at 1830 with *Llangibby Castle* and trawler *Southern Pride* at trawler speed. Our advance now about twelve and a half. So we shan't be home before 10th.

Passengers from various places, including a young Eskimo who tells good stories of the Med and particularly *Aurora*'s efforts with German Troop convoys.

Monday – Gib has really got us in the grip now – signal to proceed to Ponta Delgada with *Llangibby Castle* to pick up survivors from OWS 154, as many as possible so there must be an immense number. Let us hope we don't get into trouble ourselves. There are plenty of U-boats around there. Due to arrive 10 am Wednesday. Will presumably sail that evening so can't hope to get home now before the Tuesday.

Thursday – Arrived safely and spent twenty-four hours there amidst great merrymaking and extravagant buying. Inevitable visit from Portuguese Officer of Guard which was returned by me, wearing the Captain's stolen sword which fortunately I did not trip over. Later three of their officers came over and all talked and laughed surprisingly easily. I talked to one of them in French for some long time, he, amongst other things, telling of a U-boat survivor they had picked up who was terrified lest the British should get hold of him and torture him. Many things were bought from silk stockings to pineapples and now we are off again, due home on Tuesday.

Saturday – Weather has been very kind again, a fairly heavy sea astern and no U-boats too near according to the situation reports. Making a steady twelve which is the best *Southern Pride* can do, due back early Tuesday unless we leave her, which is suggested, and arrive four or five hours sooner, doing 13½. No news yet of what we are wanted for but *Rother* and *Spey* have not yet sailed and *Tay* is on her way back so it looks a little ominous perhaps, especially as KMF7 has sailed. *Egret* and MKF6 are four days behind us.

Interestingly the next diary entry is of our sailing from Milford Haven where we had oiled which was unusual. I can just understand the reference to the difference between life in the Army and the Navy, at any rate as I knew it. Certainly we were constantly on the move, but after all that was what ships were for. But life was never dull and I saw a lot of the world which certainly I would not have done otherwise. To have been to Curaçao, the Azores and the Mediterranean all within a few months was perhaps unusual, however. After all it even included meeting the Portuguese Navy which I have recorded. Incidentally, without practice, it is distinctly hazardous to walk down a ship's ladder wearing a sword.

It was interesting and most enjoyable to meet Alan Moorhead, who was delightful company. But as the diary records we made a shameful mess of transferring him in a whaler to another ship.

U-boats at that time in the Atlantic between England and Gibraltar were a considerable hazard as the Battle of the Atlantic was then at its height and, as I have recorded, not a life where you could afford to relax. I have, I know, referred more than once to the losses of Merchant Ships and their crews. It was not a battle which, as Churchill said, we could afford to lose. By the latter part of 1943 we were beginning to win. But, as my diary records, to have ten U-boats round you did not make for much relaxation.

What turned out to be my last sailing in *Exe* was when we escorted some tankers to Curaçao. That follows.

At last we have sailed again. As I write this we are just coming out of the entrance to Milford Haven into the swell outside. It will get worse. There has been a strong wind all night and day and it is still wild. The sky is clear but it looks as if we may well have as bad a night as we did before coming in here. I pray not. Twenty-four days at sea will be bad enough without starting badly. For that is what it is likely to be – twenty-four there and twenty-four back.

This is the one thing the Army on active service don't have to put up with – frequently setting out for overseas, never being quite sure when to be back. Through my scuttle now I can see the boom – beyond the last of the Milford cliffs. They look very bleak, and so does the sea – wild and windswept. All I can hear is the murmur of the engines, the sound of wires being secured on A gun deck above me and the occasional whistle of a man trying to appear cheerful – probably a bricklayer or a shop assistant, almost certainly not a pre-war sailor. He will feel sick and tired tonight.

Tuesday 23 – Now we are beset on all sides it seems. Everything has been delightfully peaceful until yesterday when we had a signal saying we had probably been sighted and that half a dozen U-boats between 34-30 N and 25-30 W might attempt attack. It seems they are going

136

to. Last night *Asthell Princess* straggling astern was torpedoed and now this, after HF DF fixes, *Ness* on investigating ahead sighted submarine on surface eight miles away. Afraid our whereabouts are therefore widely known. Fortunately we have oiled however, but there are still fifteen days to go.

I made the mistake of being inoculated, expecting peaceful day or two. Feel like mild attack of 'flu. But weather is good and sea calm. Unfortunately visibility is too.

Thursday 25 – They did attack at about seven in the evening before anyone realized what was happening. Apparently managed to dive under the screen, although *Ness* nearly got one. Sank two and hit two others which managed to keep going. That makes two tankers sunk and two damaged. So it went on. Expected much more last night and SM situation reported ten round us. Everyone keyed up. Strange feeling as we steamed through the convoy from astern to ahead position – dark pathetic shapes they seemed, conscious of the extreme danger they were all in.

From 7.30 until midnight the battle went on – about six being sighted and attacked by *Weston, Totland* and two others plus one batch of torpedoes. It was a fine show. They lost that round and retired. During the day we have DF'd them working up with ahead positions and it was expected that they woud try to attack by day. Nothing happened.

Submarine situation report – reduces number to seven, which at least is something.

Now it is getting dark again and everyone seems conscious of the acute contrast between the beautiful day and this sinister night. We are stationed on the port quarter this time so should have more fun. Unfortunately each night means an hour's more darkness with the waning moon. In any case they still have a fortnight with us.

No one ashore can appreciate the courage, though little alternative certainly, of the Merchant Seaman. They can do nothing. Even when they see their next ahead go up they can only steam on. Today *Totland* has been distributing one hundred and sixteen survivors amongst the twenty-nine left (twenty-eight now that the straggler for the Cape has gone).

A good example of their courage arose early this morning. One was straggling badly. Went back to warn him of necessity to keep up. Got close enough to speak through loud hailer and found she was Dutch.

137

Captain said they were doing their best but had been torpedoed in night and was worried that bulkhead might give way if he went any faster. We then saw that torpedoes had gone right through ship just astern of engine room. It was only that one bulkhead which was saving her. Clearly the torpedo had failed to explode. We wished the Dutchman well. What better example of the courage of the Merchant Navy?

Last night there were ten U-boats and ten escorts. Tonight ten – seven.

Friday 06 – Successful again. Only two managed to get up to us and they were both put down by *Landsdale,* all being quiet after about nine. But they are still with us, seven of them, and we have been DF'ing them again today, mostly on the port bow. No moon until midnight tonight.

Helped *Totland* ferry her survivors to one of the MVs this morning and fuelled from the Frenchman during the afternoon. Successful this time. Now taking up position on the quarter for the night. If we get through tonight perhaps we shall have shaken them off. Two are homeward bound anyhow

Sunday – All went well. Sighted one the next afternoon after the DF but that was apparently the last. Anyhow they have detached south-bound ships at last at 1930 tonight. Good news scene – as sun set, Commodore was seen to hoist – 'God speed, safe journey'. They were last seen going off in all directions into the night. Now our own troubles – very bad condensaritis and leaks in tanks. Only needs break down and we would be completely finished. Only another week now though. And weather gets better.

Thursday – The inevitable – orders to detach torpedoed tankers for Guantanamo, Cuba, under escort and we have been detailed, with instructions to effect repairs whilst there. But we shan't have long. We aren't due to arrive until Thursday, instead of Saturday in Curacao, which will mean only two days in perhaps. Not much news of what the place is like except that it is an American base, apparently few miles from the town – probably rather akin to Argentina.

Meanwhile the weather gets worse, but not hopelessly so. This afternoon we sight land – Antigua or Guadeloupe. Friday proceed Cuba.

Saturday (week) – Arrived there all right and had the usual wild time with an orgy of buying food in American stores. Now on our way to Curaçao to join *Weston*. Have discovered that tanks are leaking as badly as ever and that it is essential for us to dock, which is most unfortunate as it may well mean getting stuck here for a while. In company with American four stacker *Dixie*.

**Dixie was one of those destroyers from America under the Marshall Aid plan. They had four funnels. They looked, and indeed were, top heavy.**

20 March – Sailed from Cuba today after docking in floating dock for three days. Now with fast fourteen knots tanker convoy – all American – bound U.K. with the same four destroyers and others minus *Totland, Weston* and *Folkestone* who had to go on their own as they aren't fast enough. Have a strong head wind and sea now, but even so are making good thirteen. *Attacker* is with us too, which might be useful. Most of the tankers carry about eighteen thousand tons of fuel. Nine of them with us.

Sunday 21 – Nearly out into the Atlantic now. Passed the first of the islands at six and will be through the last by morning. Head wind still quite strong but making good thirteen and a half nevertheless. No news.

Plenty of U-boats ahead of us no doubt. Churchill spoke this evening of the post-war-world. Germans defeated by next year and then the Japs. It may well be difficult to get out of the Navy then.

Wednesday 14 – This evening the weather has changed completely for the colder bleaker North Atlantic. We tried to oil today from the *Esso Philadelphia* but were unsuccessful, pulling our own starboard forward bollards and parting the hose. It may become serious for it is quite possible that the weather will get no better – and worse – and we have insufficient oil to get home. On one boiler we might just do it. We pass a hundred and fifty miles off the Azores and, in any case, should not be allowed in there until our three months are up. Reported that five to ten U-boats are ahead of us. I am in bed with what Doc thinks is inflammation of the lung but is merely after-effects of the old tonsilitis.

Looks distinctly bleak out of my scuttle.

<u>Thursday 25</u> – We are oiling successfully now, using an old bit of canvas fire hose for the floating hose method astern which is slow but successful. Otherwise nothing except that lying in bed at sea is far from satisfactory. I feel extraordinarily worn out as a result of these two days.

<u>Wednesday 31</u> – All has gone extraordinarily quickly and we haven't been to action stations the whole trip. Yesterday we had orders to escort the British Channel portion south about, consisting of four out of the nine, ourselves and two others. Due Fastnet four tomorrow morning, Bristol Channel the following night and Derry early Saturday morning. But it is still possible that we shan't go there. Westerly gale still blowing hard and a heavy swell behind us.

**I have referred more than once to being ordered either to go 'south about' or 'north about'. It was a question of either coming up the Irish Channel from the south or coming down from the north, having been round the top of Ireland. Either way you were likely to come across a U-boat or two and indeed I have recorded the sad sinking of the corvette *Vervain* followed by our sinking of the U-boat, when I was in *Amethyst*. It was the fastest sinking of the war and, tragically, was to have been *Vervain*'s last duty.**

<u>2000</u> At 1700 were ordered to proceed direct to Derry, *Ness* taking the Bristol Channel portion. Should mean we shall be there by 1500 tomorrow. Going up river that night – perhaps be over the next day but why should they want us to return to Derry?

Arrived eventually at 1630 after struggling through thick mist. Discovered that we were not supposed to have left convoy until Tusker [Light House]. They had a lucky escape. Four German destroyers came out that evening and got between the SL convoy and us but sighted neither. The SL was bombed the next morning.

<u>Sunday April 18</u> – Left on Wednesday morning to swing for compasses and then proceed Larne for exercises. Arrived back Moville at 0700, did short AS and gunnery exercise and then sailed with KMF13 and WS29 on Friday. RDF broke down at last moment and we had to go up river for two hours. Finally caught up convoy after some difficulty in finding it yesterday morning. Escort of EG42 and *Rapid*, *Venomous*, *Lauderdale*, *Newcastle* and later *Charybidis*.

They are still worried about destroyers, hence the cruisers. *Newcastle* goes on to Freetown and *Charybidis* into the Med with us. It seems we may get some excitement there when we get east of Oran with torpedo bombers. Now all is quiet and weather good. Convoy of about twenty-five, including about forty to fifty thousand troops.

Tuesday 20 – All has continued very quiet and good weather. Tomorrow convoy splits and tomorrow night we go through the Straits. All seems at the moment quiet in Tunisia before the storm. It hardly looks as though that can start until after we have left. One or two U-boats have been reported and we have had HF/DF bearings. Today there were two or three contacts from ahead about the same time – we had one and *Totland*'s was confirmed but nothing came of it – seemed doubtful.

Sunday 25 – We got through to Algiers without incident in spite of all the panic about Air Attack. *Carlisle* joined during the last night and at dawn convoy and some escorts made smoke screen, completely obscuring the convoy for an hour and a half. No attack developed and we were all in by noon.

That was the only night we had in, sailing at 1830 yesterday. Algiers was in a very poor way indeed, shorter of rations by far than England and all the shops empty of everything except wine – and that only Algerian. There is meat only once a week, hardly any cheese or coffee and apparently little of anything else except green stuff. We go through Straits tonight, picking up six ships and dropping one, also three destroyers who leave again. So we are a comparatively small escort going home with no destroyers. We go to the west and are to be covered some of the way by *Bermuda*.

Rumoured that we are going to make a seaborne attack on Bizerta.

Wednesday – Weather very fine this evening for the first time, having tended to be overcast and windy from the north. No sign of any U-boats yet, but they have twice altered our course further west, presumably on account of the destroyers. *Bermuda* with a Polish destroyer is in contact.

News yesterday that '42EG will proceed Greenock for lay-over'. No one clear what that means – perhaps a spell of leave, perhaps more exercises.

<u>Thursday evening</u> – When all seemed quiet a most unexpected Focke-Wulf turned up this evening followed by two more. One had been reported on our port quarter but I took no notice of it, nor did *Wellington*, until she must have suddenly realized, for she fired two rounds at it, as it flew very low on our port beam.

Then another appeared and they flew round and round the convoy out of range for about an hour, calling up the U-boats no doubt. Finally they each dropped one bomb from a great height, well above ours and the convoy's barrage, going well wide. Now we are just waiting for something to happen – U-boats, the four destroyers or more aircraft in the morning. But we should have some of ours there too.

# CHAPTER IX

# Hospital and HMS *Dryad*

**The following entry in my diary records my experience in hospital and what followed.**

<u>May 11</u> – Here I am in the Maernskirk Hospital. What a ridiculous situation it does seem. It hardly seems possible that I should really be in hospital, supposedly sick, when I feel now as fit as I ever did. Such strange things have been said lately about me too and so many seem to have tried to cheer me up by telling obvious untruths when I am not in the least concerned, perhaps merely because I don't know the truths. And then on the other hand Doc, hearing me talk rather flippantly in the wardroom, quietly tells me in the sick bay that I am likely to be discharged from the Navy and should make sure that I get a pension. I am afraid I am the least concerned of all for there is so little I can do about it in any case.

All I have to do is relax at last in this comfortable room to myself. When a nurse showed me into it I remarked on how good it was to have a room to myself. In a pleasantly matter of fact way, she said that luckily for me the previous occupant had died the previous night!

It is difficult to believe that I shall never go to sea again, impossible that I should leave the Navy altogether. Anyhow I am very well off at the moment with this room to myself, comfortable chair and good view. Plenty of books to read. What more could I want? It will be a relief to know definitely one way or the other nevertheless.

Certainly I was very well looked after and comfortable in that hospital.

Just up the road from the hospital was a riding school where each day I was able to get a horse and greatly to enjoy myself. I wished it could have lasted longer. Tests had shown that, so they said, I had TB and was to go on indefinite sick leave. While inevitably pleased at the thought

143

of some leave, I felt very sad at leaving *Exe*. Remarkably kindly, Commander Biddulph and his wife came to see me. There was something very moving about saying goodbye after our time in *Exe* together. I was not to see him again. He was a fine example of a fearless Naval Officer who made light of any excitement, however critical. One characteristic of his was more often than not in fine weather to sit on the foreside of the bridge, facing aft. Not only did it mean he could chat more easily to the others on the bridge, who were looking forward, but also, he persuaded us, it was important that someone should keep a good look out aft.

He was a courageous, skilled and very human officer. There was something intensely sad about his funeral to which I went in, I think, 1953. I recognized no one there. No one spoke at the service of the man he was and to whom I owed so much.

Following further medical reports from various sources, naval and civilian, I was ordered six months' shore service during which time very conveniently I did the Navigation Course for Reserve Officers at *HMS Dryad* listed as (N*), the course for regular officers being listed as (N), which was followed by appointment as Navigating Officer of the new sloop *Amethyst* where I was to serve for two years until the end of the war in Europe. *Amethyst* was completing building on the Clyde. For a month or so I stayed at a nearby hotel until the time came for us to sail.

# CHAPTER X

# HMS *Amethyst*

*Amethyst*'s first night at sea on our way from the Clyde to Tobermory can now be recorded. It was my first night as Navigating Officer. It just involved sailing out of the Clyde in the evening and thence round the coast. It should have been entirely straightforward but very nearly resulted in disaster. I can still remember vividly when the First Lieutenant who was keeping the Middle Watch called me down the voice pipe in the chartroom where I slept when we were at sea to say that there was 'a lot of land about' and that I must come up to have a look. I remember very well that I said that there would be 'a lot of land about' and mentioned Rum, Muck and Eigg. But that did not satisfy him. I went up to the bridge to have a look myself. My first question was to ask if he had yet seen the light on the end of Coll. To my horror he said that they had already passed it and he pointed out the light flashing once every twenty seconds which was astern of us. My immediate reaction was that somehow we had managed to be some two hours ahead of our correct position but found it difficult to believe. One thing was certain, that, whatever the reason, we would be far ahead of our estimated time of arrival at Tobermory. The only avoidable solution at that moment was to turn back for an hour in order to waste time. I gave the necessary order and at the same time a report was made to the Captain. To my horror, when the Boatswain who was on the helm started to turn through 180 degrees I saw immediately that the giro compass was clearly out of order. At that moment the Captain came up to the bridge. As he arrived, there was the ghastly shock of seeing a rock no more than fifty yards ahead. *Amethyst* was as near as that to being wrecked on her first night at sea and incidentally my first night as navigator. All we could do was to steer due west by magnetic compass and pray we would not hit anything. By amazing good fortune we didn't. A post mortem followed.

There were two fearful reasons combined which got us into that position. First, no one had noticed the failure of the compass. In fact it was established that the warning light had come on on the bridge. The Officer of the Watch then, realizing that something was wrong with the compass, sent a sailor down to alert the seaman in charge of the electrics but by the time he got down there the light had gone out and the alarm bell which had rung below decks had stopped. The reason it had stopped was that those of the crew who were off watch below and sleeping were woken by the bell. Not knowing what was causing it one of them called out 'Stop that bloody bell' and obligingly someone else broke the circuit which not only stopped the bell but also put out the light on the bridge. The Officer of the Watch, excusably, thought all was well and that the Gyro was working correctly. But that was not the end. Sleeping in the Chart House, I knew nothing of what had been going on. Seeing that the light on the bridge had gone out, the Officer of the Watch had understandably assumed all was well and the helmsman had followed the Gyro. It was later that I was called because land appeared to be too close. The light on shore was, however, seen to be on our starboard beam but some two hours before it should have been. It is difficult for anyone who was not there to appreciate how ghastly the problem was.

We survived. While still pondering what best to do, a faint light was sighted way ahead on our starboard bow. It was flashing once every twenty seconds. We decided it must be the light we were expecting but in that event, what was the other light on our beam?

On arrival at Tobermory, the Gyro by then having been mended, we made enquiries about the other light. It turned out to be a light on the airfield in the middle of Coll with, extraordinarily, the same characteristics.

It is, I must say, a story which still haunts me. The ship which later became so famous might so easily then have been wrecked.

Again I was lucky with the captains I had. The first was Commander Tuke DSO who had been on the east coast in a destroyer. He had incidentally sunk a U-boat there, had picked up all the survivors and after the war was sent a photograph of the U-boat taken before she was sunk, signed on the back by all those whom he had rescued with a note of their thanks.

The RAF complained periodically that naval ships seemed to be quite unable to distinguish a German plane from our own. They felt that opportunities should be taken for officers to spend a few days with the Air Force at their base in Northern Ireland. Much to my annoyance, because otherwise I would have been on leave, it was suggested that I should go, which I did. The first two days really nothing happened at all, no one being interested in my presence. I made the fatal mistake of drawing the attention of the Naval Officer in charge to the fact that nothing seemed to be happening. I was with him when he telephoned the officer in charge of the Air Force base, saying that he had a young Lieutenant with him who felt that he had been ignored. The consequences were immediate. I was first sent up in a Sunderland. Although normally less exciting planes than some others, the crew alarmed me by doing a dive bombing attack on Ailsa Craig which I felt sure was something that a Sunderland would not normally do. Certainly I felt far from safe. The next day I was sent up in a Hudson bomber over the Atlantic.

That was equally alarming to me because I found the Air Force navigation distinctly uncertain. Luckily, apart from that anxiety, there was no problem as a German U-boat on that occasion was not sighted. I ought just to add that, of course, the part played by Hudsons in those days was very considerable and very valuable.

*Amethyst* joined one of the escort groups operating in the Atlantic. What followed was what we had all come to expect but by then we were getting the better of the U-boats. We were sinking more of them and losses of our ships were much reduced.

After a time in the Atlantic with all the inevitable incidents and excitements we went to the Mediterranean. It was something of a strain on my navigation but went according to plan. We operated between Beirut, Haifa and Port Said. We also went to Sicily. Some typical sailing orders follow as also does the result of a report I made to the Admiralty.

They are a good example of our movements at that time. It all put a very considerable strain on the captain of a ship. By then Commander Tuke had borne a great deal and it was not surprising that in Alexandria he was taken ill. His place as Captain of *Amethyst* was taken by Lieutenant Pengelly, a Cornishman who had risen from the lower deck. You could not have had a better captain. We came home with him

Life in the Med compared with the Atlantic was comparatively relaxed. U-boats in the area were limited and the French and Italian fleets which had caused so much trouble earlier being then inactive. Perhaps, apart from the Captain, the busiest member of the ship's company was the Navigating Officer who, as is apparent from the sailing instructions, had appreciable responsibity. Certainly I found it so. One particular occasion which I remember was when we went to Famagusta. According to the pilot for that area you were advised of a useful transit as you approached some palm trees on the starboard side of the entrance and some buildings. I spent anxious moments trying to find the palm trees which eventually I realized had been cut down.

While nothing was as bad as our first night at sea, there were always

SECRET.

(TO BE DESTROYED BY FIRE WHEN COMPLIED WITH. THESE ORDERS ARE ON
NO ACCOUNT TO BE ALLOWED TO FALL INTO THE HANDS OF THE ENEMY)

OFFICE OF SENIOR NAVAL OFFICER,
LEVANT AREA.

No. LASO/ 119           HAIFA, 10th May      194 4

### SAILING ORDERS: H.M.S. "AMETHYST".

(1)   Ship under your command being in all respects ready for sea and prepared to engage
the enemy, you are to leave Haifa at 1800C on the Wednesday 10th May
and proceed through 470 to Famagusta.

(2)   You are to escort the following ships:

| | |
|---|---|
| /M/V EOLO | to   FAMAGUSTA. |
| | to |
| | to |
| | to |
| | to |
| | to |

(3)   Your route will be in accordance with the Routeing Instructions issued to the Master(s)
of the above vessel(s).

(4)   Your time of arrival, as under, will be reported by the Senior Naval Officer, Levant
Area. (Time of Origin: S.N.O.L.A. 09 1850C )
E.T.A. at FAMAGUSTA 0658/11th May 1944.

(5)   The latest Q.B. Messages received are:—
Q.B. 299    Q.B.B. 349    Q.B.C. 888    Q.B.H. 359

(6)   You are to use your discretion in modifying these orders as may be necessary to
enable you to comply with Fighting Instructions held by you.

(7)   Receipt of these orders is to be acknowledged by signal, quoting "LASO/ 119
received".

Speed of Advance   12 knots.
Codeword NAGSHEAD/ 500

CAPTAIN
SENIOR NAVAL OFFICER,
LEVANT AREA.

TO   Commanding Officer,
H.M.S. "AMETHYST".

COPIES TO: Commanding Officer,

SECRET.

OFFICE OF SENIOR NAVAL OFFICER,
LEVANT AREA.

No. LASO/ 122                     HAIFA, 12th May           194 4

SAILING ORDERS: H.MS. AMETHYST.

(1)   Ship under your command being in all respects ready for sea and prepared to engage the enemy, you are to leave Haifa at 0700 on the 13th May , and proceed by Levant Route to Port Said taking FNS LA MOQUEUSE & REINE DES FLOTS under your orders.

(2)   You are to escort the following ships:

| | | |
|---|---|---|
| BRITISH SOLDIER. | to | PORT SAID |
| BRITISH GENIUS. | to | "       " |
| BRITISH HARMONY | to | "       " |
| REGIN | to | "       " |
| ALGORAB. | to | |
| | to | |
| | to | |

(3)   Your route will be in accordance with the Routeing Instructions issued to the Master(s) of the above vessel(s).

(4)   Your time of arrival, as under, will be reported by the Senior Naval Officer, Levant Area. (Time of Origin: S.N.O.L.A. 12 1258 )
E.T.A. at PORT SAID 0900/14th.

The latest Q.B. Messages received are:—
Q.B. 299        Q.B.B. 349        Q.B.C. 890        Q.B.H. 363

(6)   You are to use your discretion in modifying these orders as may be necessary to enable you to comply with Fighting Instructions held by you.

(7)   Receipt of these orders is to be acknowledged by signal, quoting "LASO/ 122 received".

Speed of Advance 8 knots.
Codeword MIRANDA Call Sign 718
ALGORAB will /RD at end of S/C at 0800/13th

CAPTAIN
SENIOR NAVAL OFFICER,
LEVANT AREA.

TO  Commanding Officer,
    H.M.S. AMETHYST

COPIES TO: Commanding Officer,
    F.N.S. LA MOQUEUSE.
    REINE DES FLOTS.

plenty of opportunities for extreme anxiety. One such occasion which I shall not forget was when we were bound for Malta. We had had bad weather. There had been no chance to take any sights for two days so that we were relying on Dead Reckoning when making for the swept channel without the chance to see any land until we were some way into it. The only indication of whether you had got it right or not was the depth of water. Slightly less than fifteen fathoms would be an immediate indication that you were in grave danger. I looked anxiously at the echo sounder. I was appalled to see the depth at thirteen fathoms and still dropping. I decided to give myself thirty seconds before, if the depth was still falling, telling the Captain that we must immediately go out to sea again. Clearly we were in grave danger of hitting a mine. It must surely have been the worst thirty seconds of my life. To my enormous relief, with a few seconds to spare, the depth started to creep up. Shortly afterwards we saw the light on Gozo. The ship's company did not know of the dreadful danger they had been in. I did not solve why the depth had dropped so far. I feel now I should have reported it as our subsequent position showed that we were in the channel. In fact my navigation had been rather good.

When we got home Pengelly was relieved by a great character, Commander Scott-Elliot, who had been First Lieutenant of *Zulu* at Tobruk, had gone ashore with a landing party and had been taken prisoner. He escaped from the Italians when being sent in a railway truck to Germany. He somehow got out of the bottom of the truck and managed to get over the Alps into Switzerland, whence, after some two or three months, he got home. There is a great deal that could be written about him but I must resist the temptation as he was most critical of anyone who sought to write or say anything about him. Under his command, *Amethyst* held the record for the fastest sinking of a U-boat, following the sinking of *Vervain* on our beam. It was all over in ten minutes. Half the ship's company of *Vervain* were lost. It might so easily have been ourselves – as indeed it could have been when *Exe* was relieved by another escort on the patrol off the North African coast during the Torch operation which was sunk the following night. *Vervain* had been involved in the Battle of the Atlantic almost from the start. To have been sunk in those circumstances almost within sight of the United Kingdom was very sad. There were, I am afraid, many similar incidents, both of escorts and merchant ships. I doubt if the public in the U.K. were in a position fully to appreciate it all.

Commander Scott-Elliot was awarded a Bar to his DSC which had followed the action in which he was involved off Tobruk, the Anti-

Submarine Officer was awarded a DSC and the First Lieutenant Mentioned in Dispatches. I always felt that Scott-Elliot should have had a DSO which usually followed a U-Boat sinking and that certainly the First Lieutenant should have had a DSC, having been in the Battle of the Atlantic since the beginning. But so many deserved so much. Sadly, so often distinction and courage were unknown. I could not help sometimes thinking of those who were sunk, survived in fearful conditions in open boats, but were never rescued. That is the inevitability of war.

It was on our return from the Mediterranian that we joined the escort group EG42. The Senior Officer was Commander Leftwich in *Hart* and his Navigation Officer my brother-in-law to be, John Ellyatt.

One thing I remember about Scott-Elliot was his insistance that every evening at 1730 I should meet him on the foredeck when we should walk – or his words were 'weave' – up and down for half an hour quite regardless of the weather. Indeed there were times when it was distinctly hazardous but he insisted nevertheless. It was typical of a remarkable man for whom I continued until his death in 1999 to have considerable admiration and who became a great friend.

On Sundays, whenever the weather and the state of play with U-boats permitted, we used to have a church service, so called. All it in fact amounted to was singing the National Anthem and then, totally inappropriately in a church service, Scott-Elliot always asked me, when we had got them, to read the Weekly Intelligence Reports. It was a strange scene to have the ship's company assembled on deck, usually in distinctly rough weather, and that the Weekly Intelligence Reports should be deemed suitable for a Sunday morning service.

One other thing I can record is that when we were chasing a U-boat off the west coast of Ireland, he was, I thought, paying insufficient attention to the danger of being too close to the rocks. I dared to say to him 'I don't think this is wise, sir,' to which he replied, 'Pilot, you will never get anywhere in this life if you only do what is wise'. That incident is referred to in the remarkable obituaries which appeared in the *Daily Telegraph* and *The Times*. He was indeed a great man.

There were at least two further occasions when we attacked U-boats and hopefully sunk them. On one occasion we did so in conjunction with some of the other escorts in EG22. There was evidence of a successful sinking. A further occasion was when we attacked another U-boat ourselves. We certainly assumed the U-boat had been sunk when there was a very considerable explosion and oil on the surface. But by a remarkable coincidence Scott-Elliot was at a lecture after the war at which a U-boat commander was present and spoke of this particular occasion. He disclosed that he had been on the bottom near a sunk ship which was what had exploded. He escaped.

. Reading these diaries again, I am reminded of so many incidents which are not recorded. For one reason or another I shall not forget them. No doubt others who served in those ships will remember them too.

I shall not, of course, ever forget the attack by the *Hipper* on Christmas Day 1940. There were many others which I remember vividly but for different reasons. The emotion generated by some experiences is still there. There was, for instance, the time we left Gibraltar with a small convoy of larger ships than usual when the U-boats were in considerable numbers in the area approachng the Straits. It had become a graveyard evidenced by empty lifeboats, life jackets and, worst of all, dead bodies. Those aboard the ships we were to convoy were largely made up of troops returning from the Torch operation and Naval nursing staff.

At that time on *Exe* we still had Commander Biddulph in command. Something he always enjoyed was to play sentimental tunes over our loud hailer when leaving harbour. In particular I remember leaving Gibraltar as we played 'I'm dreaming of a White Christmas'. As we sailed past some of the ships, they lined their decks and waved. Two nights later at least two were sunk with fearful loss of life. But I shall never forget. They thought they were going home. Instead they are buried at sea.

It was while I was in *Amethyst* when we used to come into Plymouth periodically that I felt I just could not wait any longer to propose to John Ellyatt's sister, Mary, the boating Wren, then a Petty Officer, whom I had first met when in *Clematis* but had had very little chance to see thereafter. It was inevitable that when I had the chance to see her more I would want to persuade her to marry me. And so indeed it was. As soon as I got back to *Amethyst* again one evening just before we were due to sail with another convoy across the Atlantic, I managed to get the message to her on her boat (which follows and which I found she had kept). The following morning when we were just beginning to leave the dock, Mary appeared on the dockside, waved to me and held her thumbs up. *Amethyst* left Plymouth with me a happy man.

We then agreed, miraculously, by correspondence which we managed to exchange that we should aim at a wedding when we came into Liverpool for our next boiler clean. Mary knew that it usually took four or five weeks to take a convoy out and to bring one back and had managed to alert her parents to the probability of a decision to fix the actual date as soon as we got back to Liverpool. It was indeed when we next came in that I sent her the telegram which follows. Somehow her parents had managed to be prepared for it, guessing at the sort of date.

## NAVAL MESSAGE.

S. 1320b

M11255/D7843 500,000 pads 8/44 MoO (N) 12-6597

| For use in Signal Department only | | | | |
|---|---|---|---|---|

| Originators Instructions (Indication of Priority, Intercept Group, etc.) | | | Codress/Plaindress | No. of Groups |
|---|---|---|---|---|

TO: A and Wren.

FROM: Guess Who?

| | | | | | | | |
|---|---|---|---|---|---|---|---|
| | | | | | | | 5 |
| | | | | | | | 10 |
| | Will you please? | | | I | don't | think | 15 |
| | I can wait after all. | | | Reply | by | | 20 |
| | thumbs up or DOWN. | | | | | | 25 |
| | | | | | | | 30 |
| | | | Johnny | | | | 35 |
| | | | | | | | 40 |
| | | | | | | | 45 |
| | | | | | | | 50 |

| P/L Code or Cypher | Time of Receipt | Despatch | Operator | P.O.O.W. | Date |
|---|---|---|---|---|---|

---

| Charges to pay s. d. | | POST ✹ OFFICE | No. 11 |
|---|---|---|---|
| RECEIVED | | TELEGRAM | OFFICE STAMP |

Prefix   Time handed in.   Office of Origin and Service Instructions.   Words.

From   TA   3·32 m   2·36 pm ⅃ V/T   15   To _____ m

Priority Belyatt 11 The Strand Shalden N. Torquay

Leave starting today suggest wedding Monday
John

51/8671 MP

For free repetition of doubtful words telephone "TELEGRAMS ENQUIRY" or call, with this form at office of delivery. Other enquiries should be accompanied by this form and if possible, the envelope   8 or C

It was enormously kind that so many officers and ship's company, including Scott-Elliot and the Captain of *Hart*, should have managed to come to Shaldon that Monday in February.

The banns had been read while I was away. We were married in St. Peter's Church at Shaldon.

We had three days' honeymoon, the last a night in Birkenhead. We sailed in the morning. I was wearing some fur-lined boots which Mary had given me. As we passed the Royal Liver Buildings, Ninian Scott-Elliot spotted them as we stood on the bridge and said, 'I suppose that is what marriage does for you'. All I can say is that they were mighty useful in the cold of the North Atlantic.

Mary had by then returned to her Wren duties in Plymouth as coxswain of a boat based in the dockyard at Devonport. There then followed further convoys across the Atlantic. It did not occur to Mary or to me that we might in *Amethyst* be overcome by some disaster, and that I would not return. The European war ended. It was then that I was appointed to the staff at *Dryad*, finally being demobilized in March 1946. They had been remarkable years.

Looking back at one's days in the three ships, *Clematis, Exe* and *Amethyst*, whilst similar in many ways, life was still very different. There was nothing to compare with life in the North Atlantic in a ship as small as a corvette and facing U-boat warfare in those days when losses were so appalling. Yet there was nothing to compare with North Africa and the very different life in *Exe*. Again the losses were very heavy, but all on a different scale. That was true also of *Amethyst* in the Atlantic and Mediterranean. In both the possibility of disaster, either from bombing or U-boats, was always present. It was not by chance that she sank two, or very possibly three, U-boats. She, too, had more than one outstanding Captain. The courage of her ship's company was in the best tradition, as it always had been. There is so much that I might add to these diaries, but I hope the distinction of three fine ships is adequately reflected in what I have said.

The picture of that enormous convoy and the possibilities of disaster will always stick in my mind, as will that picture of leaving Gibraltar on Christmas Eve with the homeward-bound ships which ran into U-boats and disaster when only two days out. I have recorded our playing 'I'm dreaming of a White Christmas' on our loud hailer as we all left. Two days later all was destroyed for so many.

I know that throughout my diaries and my comments I have said how lucky I was in many ways, in the ships in which I served and the Captains, brother officers and crew whom I met and got to know so well. Without exception, it was they who made life not only such a valuable experience and such good training for life ahead but also so remarkably enjoyable in a strange way. I certainly would not have wanted to miss it. No doubt service in the Army and the Air Force provoked the same feelings but neither of the other two services could surely quite substitute for one's feelings about the ships in which you served. We were enormously lucky in *Clematis*, *Exe* and *Amethyst* but, whilst recalling our lives in them, at the same time I remember the ghastly moments which overtook so many of our fellow ships and nearly overtook us. Nothing will ever remove from my mind my feelings at the time about the loss of life in those ships which were sunk in company with us. To have said I was lucky is an understatement.

Yet I would not have wanted to substitute that life for any other. I believe my shipmates felt the same. A reunion as we all get older is a moving occasion, as it is bound to be. If any of them should read what I have written I just hope they will feel as I do. I shall remember them all with pride and those of my friends who were lost with great sadness.

It was I who had the luck. There were those three particular incidents when luck played its outstanding part. Clearly the first, and the one which stands out above all others, was Christmas Day 1940 when only one direct hit from the *Hipper* would have been the end of *Clematis*. In *Exe* there were again many opportunities for disaster to strike but one occasion which sticks in my mind was when we left the patrol off Arzeu during the North African campaign and the escort which took our place was sunk the following night. Finally it could so easily have been *Amethyst* which was sunk and not *Vervain* when escorting the convoy approaching the Irish coast.

Luck could not have been more on my side than it was.

# CHAPTER XI

# U-Boat Surrender

It was hard to accept that the war was really over when we had the signal on 5 May. At the time we were in the approaches to the Channel, still alert to the possibility of U-boats. The sinking of *Vervain* did not seem long ago. When we then had a signal to board any U-boat that might be sighted and which should be flying a black flag to indicate the intention to surrender, we found it difficult to believe. But while we were just beginning to realize what was going on, that was just what we saw a few miles away. It was in fact the first U-boat to surrender. It had actually already done so to *Magpie* who signalled us with her position to take over. A whaler was quickly launched and the Captain asked me to board her as I could speak German and to check there were no explosives on board. It hardly seemed it could be true. I remember well that although the sea was comparatively calm it was still distinctly difficult to get on board. The crew behaved well and I was shown down below. I was then immediately conscious of a very different character from the others, without doubt the dangerous Nazi who was on board to ensure that there would, so far as he could prevent it, be no question of surrender. I felt much safer when I had got up to the conning tower again.

The Captain could not have been more dignified or have behaved better. I told him we were to go to Portland. Although they had been at sea for two weeks, both he, particularly, and his crew were all in their uniforms and clean-shaven. It was impressive.

As we were coming in to Portland he handed me his binoculars, saying that they would be no use to him any more. Sadly, having told the two sailors who came with me that we were not to take anything from the U-boat, I felt bound to hand them back again. I wished so much all those years later that I could have had them to hand back to him at the Reunion. As it was, everything was taken by a Polish boarding party.

We came alongside a jetty and I said goodbye to him. I gave him a note of my name and address, telling him to let me know if there should be anything I might be able to do to help. I then said goodbye and did not see him again for fifty years.

My three months on the staff at HMS *Dryad* to which I was then appointed were both interesting and enjoyable and provided in a strange way a valuable culmination of those six years in the Royal Navy. No one could have been kinder than the three Commanders on the staff who took a helpful interest in the career which lay ahead of me. In many ways they were very constructive and again I was lucky. Eventually the end came when I was given a civilian suit, a hat, shoes and a raincoat. I took them with me when I cycled on an old lady's bicycle to Havant station. I had imagined that in some way the trumpets would blow as I left the Navy. Inwardly they did, for so many varied reasons.

My days at *Dryad* provided a most excellent interlude between the end of the war in Europe and my return to civilian life. The great bonus was that it enabled Mary and me to live in digs nearby. Indeed it was our first chance to live together. We both remember very well the cottage at Southwick. One very good feature was a feather bed which could hardly have been more detached from my days in a ship. Not surprisingly the lavatory was at the bottom of the garden, and quite a large garden too.

There was plenty of time in which to reflect on our wartime years. For my part, I was very conscious that the war should have provided me with a wonderful wife and the valuable experience – for so it was – of life in the Navy, both in those merchant ships and the three escorts. Of course, again I was enormously lucky, not just to have survived but also in meeting all those who served with me. I remember the ships very clearly, but particularly I remember those who served with me. I wish so much that I could see them all again.

I know that throughout my diaries and recollections of what we did I have said how lucky I had been. The fact is that is just what I was. Now some fifty-six years later I am increasingly conscious of it as each year passes.

# CHAPTER XII

# Reunion after Fifty Years

It was fifty years later that I had a letter from Heinz Schroeteler, the captain of the U-boat which had surrendered to us, asking me if my wife and I would like to come to Germany for their Reunion in May 1995 near Düsseldorf. We could not refuse.

It was a moving occasion. It took place in the captain's studio, he having become a well-known painter and sculptor. We were met at the airport by the engineer and the captain's wife who then drove us to the captain's studio at Bochum. When we were shown into it, they all stood up and clapped. There then followed introductions to all the crew and officers who still survived and a speech by the captain to which I replied in German, having been helped with it by a German friend in England. There was much talk and singing to tunes from an accordion, the whole atmosphere being at times distinctly moving as well known songs were played and sung.

It must have been the combination of skill and luck which had enabled Schroeteler to survive the war in the Atlantic. I found he had been in U-boats the whole war, having been a regular officer in the German navy. I asked him how he had managed to survive. He said that for the previous eighteen months, when ordered to a particular position in the Atlantic, he had in fact never gone there, knowing that we had broken their code and that we would have been waiting for him.

Having arrived on a Friday evening, we left on Sunday morning, having been very well looked after on the Saturday. Again the player of the accordion played sentimental tunes as they all walked out with us to the waiting car. The captain was there. We said goodbye. It was difficult to believe that fifty years previously our job was to kill each other. I found it hard not to display the emotion which I felt. I believe he felt the same. The futility of war could not have been better illustrated.

The Battle of the Atlantic is not forgotten and certainly not by those who took part in it. Churchill is on record as saying that if we had lost the Battle of the Atlantic we would have lost the war.

There was a reunion in June 2001 which was recorded in the *Navy News*, headed:-

## ATLANTIC VETERANS RETURN TO LIVERPOOL

Veterans who fought in the Battle of the Atlantic gathered in Liverpool to commemorate the longest running Naval engagement of World War II.

More than 350 veterans took part in a march through the city which was at the heart of the struggle against Nazi domination of the Atlantic.

The Battle of the Atlantic kept open supplies of men, food and fuel which were essential to Britain's survival, and Liverpool played a major role. More than 1,000 convoys used the port during the war and, in 1941, Liverpool, became the Headquarters of the Western Approaches Command.

It would be sad if it were to be forgotten.

# Index

*Abasso* (merchant ship), 84
*Aberdeen*, HMS, 66
*Achilles*, HMS, loss of, 44
*Adda* (merchant ship), 74
*Admiral Scheer* (German battle cruiser), 30, 41, 46, 47–48, 52, 62
*Albatross*, HMS, 127
Alexander, A.V., First Lord of the Admiralty, 31–32
Algiers, 123, 126, 141
*Altmark*, torpedoed, 127–28
*Amaranthus*, HMS, 68, 70
*Amazon*, HMS, 127, 128, 129
*Amethyst*, HMS (sloop), 2, 6, 23, 140, 144, 145–50, 152, 154, 155
sailing orders, *148, 149*
*Aministan* (merchant ship), 14
*Anchusa*, HMS, 59, 68, 69, 70, 98
*Argonaut*, HMS, 133
*Argus*, HMS, 127, 129
Arzeu, Algeria, 126, 128, 155
*Ashbury* (merchant ship), 63
*Asphodel*, HMS, 29, 67, 69, 70, 88, 90, 101, 112
Azores, 114, 115, 116
at Freetown, 109
*Assyrian*, torpedoed, 75
*Aster*, HMS, 74
*Asthell Princess* (merchant ship), 137
Atlantic, Battle of, 121, 136, 158–59
reunion (2001), 159
*Atlantic Coast* (merchant ship), 101–02
*Attacker*, HMS, 139
*Aurora*, HMS, 52, 53, 126, 135
*Ausonia* (Armed Merchant Cruiser), 29
*Avenger*, HMS, 127, 130, 131
*Avondale*, HMS, 130
Azores, 33, 111, 113–14, 115, 116

*Banff*, HMS, 129, 130, 132–33
Barker, Stoker, 45
Bathurst, Gambia, 54, 63–66, 74
*Belgravian* (merchant ship), 75, 87
*Bermuda*, HMS, 141
*Berwick*, HMS, 29, 30, 31, 32, 33, 94
*Beverley* (US destroyer), 29, 115–16
Biddulph, Commander, 122, 144, 152
*Birmingham*, HMS, 50, 78
*Bismark*, and sinking of *Hood*, 69
*Biter*, 123, 124
*Blean the Hunt*, (merchant ship), 132
Blyden, Edward, 76
Boarding party, French convoy, 70–72
*Bonaventure*, HMS, 29–33, 57, 94
Bowles, Seaman, 94
*Bridgwater*, HMS, 66, 101
*Brilliant*, HMS, 98, 112, 126
*Britannia*, HMS, 54, 94
*Britannic* troop ship, 96
*British Gernadier*, torpedoed, 68
*Broadway*, torpedoed, 114
*Broke*, HMS, 127, 130
*Bulalo* (merchant ship), 52, 53, 132
Burgess, Lt, RNVR, 81
Burroughs, Rear Admiral, 132

*Calendula*, HMS, 69, 109
Canary Islands, 113
Cape Verde Islands, 72–73
*Carlisle*, HMS, 141
Castle, Peter, 78, 79
*Charles Plumier* (French ship), 37
*Charybdis*, HMS, 140
*City of Durham*, HMS, 69, 70
*City of Edinburgh*, HMS, 130
*Clacton*, HMS, 127
*Clare*, HMS, 124–25, 129

Cleeves, Commander Yorke McLeod, 25,
    29, 31, 104, 117
    Memorial address, 119–20
*Clematis*, HMS (corvette), 2, 6, 22, 154
    Atlantic convoys, 25–32
    and capture of French convoy, 70–72
    ode to, 23, 24–25
    verse on *Hipper* incident, 30–31
*Clover*, HMS, 112
Clyde, River, 129, 145–46
Cochrane, Admiral, 69
*Columbine*, HMS, 66, 67, 70, 88, 112,
    115, 116
    at Freetown, 108, 109
Commons, Acting Petty Officer John, 26,
    27–28
Convoys, 7, 35–37, 95
    Atlantic, 25–32
    Cape Town, 101
    Freetown Escort Group, 41
    North Atlantic, 136–40
    South Atlantic, 106–07
    Takoradi, 101
*Cornwall*, HMS, 63
Corvettes, convoy duty, 35–37
*Cothay*, HMS, 90
Crete, news of invasion, 67, 68
Cripps, S.L., 69, 76, 81–82, 83, 90, 91,
    94, 97
    Takoradi, 92, 93
*Criton*, HMS, 97
*Crocus*, HMS, 92, 94, 98
*Croome*, HMS, 114
Cuba 138–39
Curaçao, 136, 139
*Curacao*, HMS, 50
*Cyclamen*, HMS, 38, 46, 47, 54–55, 56
    at Freetown, 108, 109, 110
    off West Africa, 6, 74, 87–88, 98, 112

*Daily Herald*, article on convoys, 35–37
Dakar, occupied by Germans, 69
*Delphinium*, HMS, 52
*Deptford* (merchant ship), 95
*Diamond*, HMS, 61
Diggles, Lt, 81
*Dixie* (American destroyer), 139
*Dorsetshire*, HMS, 63, 69, 98
*Dragon*, HMS, 63
*Dryad*, HMS, 144, 154, 157
*Dunbar*, HMS, 130
*Dunedin*, HMS, 29, 30, 31, 60
*Dunoon*, HMS, 54, 77
*Dunottar Castle*, (merchant ship), 54, 78

*Eagle*, HMS, hockey match, 95–96
East, Major, 85
*Edinburgh Castle*, HMS, 45, 47, 51, 52,
    77, 79, 88
    at Freetown, 89, 108
*Egret*, HMS, 129, 130, 132–33, 134
Ellyatt, John, 22, 33, 151
    broken toe, 89–90, 95
    in Gibraltar, 37–38
Ellyatt, Mary, 22, 120, 157
    proposal of marriage to, 152, 153
    wedding, 152, 153, 154
*Elmdene* (merchant ship) 74
Emden, A.B., 8
*Empire Trooper* (troop ship), 29, 31,
    32–34
*Empress of Australia*, 45–46
*Esso Philadelphia* (tanker), 139
*Exe* (frigate), 2, 6, 121–22, 152, 154, 155

Famagusta, Cyprus, 147
*Farndale*, HMS, 130
*Felixstowe*, HMS, 127
*Fishguard*, HMS, 133
*Fleur de Lys*, loss of, 114
*Folkestone*, HMS, 139
Forte, R., 81
*Foxhound*, HMS, 54
Freaker, Commander, 121
Free French, 65–66, 100–101, 102
Freetown, 41, 43–44, 45, 51, 56, 88,
    107–08
    sailing boat acquired, 78–79
French Air Force (Vichy), 37
French Navy (Vichy), 42, 70, 93, 122,
    126
Friedmann, Mr, Freetown, 80–81
*Furious*, HMS, 50, 52–53

*Gardenia*, HMS, 126, 130
*Geranium*, HMS, 38
*Germania* (German tanker), 133
Germany
    expulsion of Jews, 86
    school in, 1–2
Gibraltar, 15, 127–28, 130–31, 134–35
    first voyage to, 9–14
    shore leave, 37–39
*Glasgow*, HMS, 47, 52
*Gloisdale*, HMS, 127
*Gneisenau* (German battle cruiser), 50,
    51, 54, 62
*Godetia*, HMS, 66
Greece, news of, 58, 60

Greenfield, Lt, 65, 81
Guantanamo, Cuba, 138

Hartland, HMS, 5, 122, 126, 127, 128,
    129, 130
Hecla, HMS, 131
Hedgehogs (anti-submarine armament),
    121–22
Hill, Charles, 23
Hipper (German battle cruiser), 33, 41,
    51, 52, 95, 152, 155
Hockey matches
  Freetown, 81, 84, 90, 95–96
  Lagos, 103, 106
Hood, HMS, sinking of, 69

Ibis, HMS, 129, 130

Jamaica, 125
Japan, rumours of, 86, 87
Jervis Bay (merchant ship), 87

Karabagh, SS, 19
Kelly, HMS, 75
King Alfred naval base (Brighton), 21, 22
Kingston Hill (merchant ship), 72–73
Konakry, Vichy French concentration
    camp, 91, 96–97

Lagos, 58, 101–07
Landsdale, HMS, 138
Larne, Northern Ireland, 140
Lauderdale, HMS, 140
Lecky, Lt, 83, 84, 92, 93
Leftwich, Commander, 151
Liverpool, 152, 154
  Battle of Atlantic reunion (2001), 159
Llangibby Castle (merchant ship), 135
London (transport ship), 75
Londonderry, 134, 140
Londonderry, HMS, 112
Loyal, HMS, 134

McWhinnie, A.J., on corvettes, 35–37
Maernskirk Hospital, 143–44
Magpie, HMS, 156
Malaya, HMS, 50, 51–52
Malta, 150
Manxman, torpedoed, 130
Marguerite (merchant ship), 52, 53, 63
Marlon (Armed Merchant Cruiser), 42
Marne, HMS, 131
Martin, HMS, 130

Maundrell, Captain, (Commodore), 9
Mauritius, HMS, 52, 53, 56, 64
Mediterranean, 147, 150–51
Merchant Service, 19, 136
  courage of, 137–38
Mignonette, HMS, 82, 86, 87
Milford Haven, 135, 136
Milford, HMS, 46, 90
Miller, Surgeon Lieutenant, 15–16
Mohawk, HMS, 58
Monsarrat, Nicholas, 6, 22
Moorhead, Alan, 134, 136
Moreton Bay, 70, 86, 87
Morgan, Inspector of Police (Lagos), 105
Mountbatten, Lord Louis, 75
Mull, Isle of, 23, 145–46

Navigation, 2, 5, 145–46
Ness, HMS, 137, 140
New Northland (merchant ship), 74, 75
Newall, Major Thomas, 38
Newcastle, HMS, 140, 141
Newfoundland, Placentia Bay, 25–28
Normandie (merchant ship), 74
North Africa, 122, 123–24, 125, 129, 130
North Western Approaches, 109, 110

Operation Torch, 5, 122, 125–29
Oran, Algeria, 122, 123, 125, 126–27
Orbita (merchant ship), 129
Osiris, HMS, 38–39
Oxfordshire (hospital ship), 59, 68, 75,
    82, 89–90

Palmer, Peter (brother), 2, 8, 123
  letters, 49–50, 77
Parrot, on Clematis, 117, 118
Pengelly, Lieutenant, 147, 150
Peters, Captain, 128
Phoebe, HMS, 50
Picotex, lost, 99
Placentia Bay, Newfoundland, 25–28
Plymouth, 120, 152
Ponta Delgada, Azores, 33, 111, 113–14
Porcupine, torpedoed, 131
Portland, 156–57
Portuguese Navy, 135, 136
Prinz Eugen, 116
Prison camps
  for French (Sierra Leone), 91
  Vichy French (Konakry), 96–97

Quickmatch, 129, 130

Rapello (merchant ship), 52
Rapid, HMS, 140
Redoubt, HMS, 130
Reno de Pacifico (merchant ship), 129
Renown, HMS, 50
Repulse, HMS, 50, 52–53
Revenge, HMS, 98
Richards, Lt, 65
RNVR, application to, 2, 3–4, 5
Rodney, HMS, 51, 126
Rommel, General Erwin, 123, 125
Rother, HMS, 123, 124, 132, 135
Royal Air Force, 146–47
Runswick (merchant ship), 16

Sailing boat, acquired near Freetown,
    78–79
Sailing Orders
    Amethyst, 148, 149
    Gibraltar to Freetown, 40
St Briac, 48–49
Samuel Chase (merchant ship), 129
Scharnhorst (German battle cruiser), 50,
    51, 54
Schroeteler, Heinz, U-boat commander,
    158
Scott-Elliot, Commander Ninian, 150–52,
    154
Scythia, HMS, 75, 77
Sennen, HMS, 132, 133
Sewell, Petty Officer James, 26, 27–28
Shaldon, St Peter's Church, 154
Sheffield, HMS, 123, 124
Singapore, 86
Southern Pride (trawler), 135
Southwick, cottage at, 157
Spey, HMS, 132, 135
Stephenson, Admiral, 23
Stork, HMS, 29, 112, 115, 116, 131
Surat, torpedoed, 62
Survivors, search for, 130–31, 135, 152
Swale, HMS, 123, 127, 129

Takoradi, 58, 89, 92–93
Tanatside, HMS, 129, 130, 132, 133
Tangier, 14, 15, 41, 125
Tay, HMS, 131, 133, 135
Taylor, Annie, 79
Test, HMS, 133
Tobermory, Isle of Mull 23, 145–46

Tobruk, 44, 150
Totland, HMS, 137, 138, 139, 141
Tourot, Capitaine, 65
Tuke, Commander, 146
Turs (French ship), 72
Tynwald, HMS, 129, 130

U-boats, 26, 29, 115–16, 151
    around Cape Verde Islands, 72, 97
    Atlantic convoys, 26, 28–29
    German navy reunion (1995), 158
    North Atlantic, 136–37, 138, 139, 147
    off West Africa, 111
    surrender of, 156–57
    U123 26, 29
United States, declaration of war, 103
United States Navy, 59
Unwin, Commander, 129

Vaclite (merchant ship), sunk, 11, 12
Vanoc (merchant ship), 131–32
Vansittart, HMS, 77
Velox (merchant ship), 74, 95, 98, 111
Venomous, HMS, 140
Vervain, HMS (corvette), 140, 150, 155
Viceroy of India, torpedoed, 127
Vindictive, HMS, 76, 78, 82
    hockey matches, 81, 84, 90
Voltaire (Armed Merchant Cruiser), 61,
    94
Vulliamy, John, 77

Walney, HMS, 5, 122, 126, 127, 129,
    130
Waranga (merchant ship), 16, 19
Wear, HMS, 131
Wellington, HMS, 29, 112, 115–16, 142
Westcott, 125
Weston, HMS, 137, 139
Wild Swan, HMS, 77
Williams, Lieutenant, RN, 39
Wishart, HMS, 98, 132
Woodruff, HMS, 82, 85, 86, 87
Woodruffe, Lieutenant Commander, 128
Wrestler, HMS, 98, 111, 127–28, 129
Wyvern, HMS, 77

Yeoman (merchant ship), 72

Zulu, HMS, 150